THE FUTURE OF WORK

Studies in Critical Social Sciences Book Series

Haymarket Books is proud to be working with Brill Academic Publishers (www.brill.nl) to republish the *Studies in Critical Social Sciences* book series in paperback editions. This peer-reviewed book series offers insights into our current reality by exploring the content and consequences of power relationships under capitalism, and by considering the spaces of opposition and resistance to these changes that have been defining our new age. Our full catalog of *SCSS* volumes can be viewed at https://www.haymarketbooks .org/series_collections/4-studies-in-critical-social-sciences.

THE FUTURE OF WORK

Super-exploitation and Social Precariousness in the 21st Century

ADRIÁN SOTELO VALENCIA

Translated by
Amanda Latimer

Haymarket
Books
Chicago, IL

First published in 2015 by Brill Academic Publishers, The Netherlands.
© 2016 Koninklijke Brill NV, Leiden, The Netherlands

Published in paperback in 2018 by
Haymarket Books
P.O. Box 180165
Chicago, IL 60618
773-583-7884
www.haymarketbooks.org

ISBN: 978-1-60846-710-5

Trade distribution:
In the U.S. through Consortium Book Sales, www.cbsd.com
In Canada, Publishers Group Canada, www.pgcbooks.ca
In the UK, Turnaround Publisher Services, www.turnaround-uk.com
In all other countries by Publishers Group Worldwide, www.pgw.com

Cover design by Jamie Kerry of Belle Étoile Studios and Ragina Johnson.

This book was published with the generous support of Lannan Foundation
and the Wallace Action Fund.

Printed in Canada by union labor.

10 9 8 7 6 5 4 3 2 1

Library of Congress Cataloging-in-Publication Data is available.

To Mary: For accompanying me on this journey through life

∵

Contents

PART 2
The World of Work in the 21st Century

Foreword

Every so often, a book comes along that shakes up the way we look at the world. *The Future of Work: Super-exploitation and Social Precariousness in the 21st Century* is one of those. It is a treatise that explores an inexorable transformation taking place in the world of work under the weight of a global capitalist order in crisis. At issue is the standard of living and ultimately even the survival prospects of the immense majority of humanity in what is shaping up as an antipodal conflict of epochal proportions.

Writing now four decades after Harry Braverman penned his legendary *Labor and Monopoly Capital*, Adrián Sotelo Valencia has boldly stepped forward to bring us to a new level. What has been missing in the critical sociology of work literature is an analysis that can adequately capture the shifting systemic contradictions of the capitalist labour process across the entire global process of accumulation. In this work, Sotelo follows in the footsteps of seminal Marxist theorists such as Gramsci, Mészáros and Marini. His aim is a fully systemic analysis of capital's morphology as it completes the transition from the once 'stable' Fordist social organization of work to the signature hyper-exploited labour and precarious forms of work in the neoliberal-led era.

How to grasp the complexity of this integral process, a moving target, has proven to be elusive in an era where increasing globalization periodically appears to grant capital a new lease on life. Sotelo, a distinguished Mexican sociologist, is well equipped for this challenge. His previous work has earned him substantial recognition as an international expert on labour in the context of the social relations of dependency. In developing a powerful optic from the global South, Sotelo is already regarded as a foremost expert in interpreting the work of the influential Brazilian Marxist Ruy Mauro Marini, one of the pioneers of advanced dependency theory.

In the present work, Sotelo puts forward a compelling structural explanation of the stalling incapacity of capital to maintain profitability in the 21st century context of global accumulation. Following the pioneering work of Mészáros, Sotelo posits the structural limits of capital by reminding us of its absolute dependence upon labour. Moreover, he demonstrates how in the attempt to confront its structural crisis, a crisis of the realisation of relative surplus value, capital has resorted to an increasingly systemic reliance upon super-exploitation, the latter following the distinctive formulation first introduced by Marini as a corrective to Marx.

Backed into a corner and saddled with a strategy that assumes varied forms of reductions of workers' rights and contraction of the social safety net, the contradictory practices of capital act to suffocate system stability by both seeking and yet actively preventing a systemic rescue of its own social metabolism. The stage is set where only labour can be understood as the potentially revolutionary agency of social transformation in its antagonistic relationship with capital. Just as Gramsci, Lúkacs and others argued that, in an earlier era, the creation of counter-hegemonic social mediations ultimately arises out of ongoing social resistance within actually existing historical social contexts.

Sotelo's critical analysis amounts to a structural anatomy of the super-exploitation of labour in which he masterfully demonstrates the fruits of a rigorous Marxist analysis, emphasizing its applicability to those global regions locked into the structures of capitalist dependency. Just as the evolving nature of dependent capitalist social relations have disproportionally intensified exploitation in order to merely maintain capital accumulation, the necessity for repression in support of increasing precarity is drawn into sharp relief. In the final analysis, Sotelo builds a deeply structural analysis of super-exploitation that links the rise of the social precariat in core locations, such as Europe and the US, to ever more extreme surplus extraction processes found throughout periphery and semi-periphery nations, all in a global context where the shift of emphasis to fictitious and speculative capital has coincided with the creation of surplus populations destined for migration to the global North.

The *Studies in Critical Social Sciences* series is pleased to make available this important work of Adrián Sotelo Valencia to the English-speaking world and with it present a voice from the global South that offers important tools for forging a path to another possible world.

R. A. Dello Buono
Manhattan College, New York City

List of Tables and Figures

Tables

Figures

List of Abbreviations

C	Commodity
c	Constant capital
lp	Labour power
lpr	Labour process
ml	Means of labour
mp	Means of production
obj	Object of labour
pf	Productive forces
sv/v	Rate of surplus value
nt	Socially-necessary labour time
st	Surplus labour time
vc	Valorising capital
v	Variable capital

Introduction

No sooner had the negative effects of the 2007 crack in the global economy and the collapse of the US investment bank *Lehman Brothers* taken hold when, a year later, a new financial crack appeared, stemming from economic complications which would lead the US government to increase its debt ceiling so as to avoid the fall of the largest economy on the planet into insolvency for the first time in its history. The straw that broke the camel's back was the lowering of the US credit rating for its long-term debt—again for the first time—from AAA (the highest rating granted by the credit rating agencies to national sovereign debt) to AA+ by Standard & Poor's, over concerns regarding the government's budget deficit and growing national debt. According to World Bank figures, the national debt had reached the sum of US$14.58 trillion in 2010 and, according to projections by the US Treasury Department, would reach $15 trillion (102 percent of GDP) by the end of 2011.[1] In general terms (in other words, in relation to the entire capitalist system), resources had been injected into the banking and financial system in the amount of approximately 20 trillion dollars; approximately a third of the global product, in the amount of $50 trillion, had been completely insufficient to ameliorate and overcome the crisis.[2]

The limited cuts in public spending approved by the US House of Representatives, compared to the $4 trillion reduction over 10 years recommended by Standard & Poor's, was the main trigger of the downgrade of US treasury debt. Nonetheless, so strong was the measure that, according to the international press, by June of the same year the outflow of capital abroad reached $45 billion; while in the first week of August it rose to $82 billion on financial markets due to fears and uncertainties over the US situation following the announcement of the downgrade.

---

1   "Standard & Poor's priva a EE UU de la tripla A por su 'improvisada política fiscal'," *El País*, 6 August 2011, accessed 21 July 2014, available http://economia.elpais.com/economia/2011/08/06/actualidad/1312615974_850215.html. With 269 votes in favour and 161 against (95 from the so-called "left" of the Democratic Party and 66 from the ultraconservatives of the Tea Party movement), the US Congress approved a plan to raise the debt ceiling to US$14.3 billion. ECLAC has issued its own assessment in *Latin America and the Caribbean in the World Economy 2010–2011: The Region in the Decade of the Emerging Economies*, Santiago de Chile, United Nations, 2011 [TN: The text uses American standard determinations of billion (10^9) and trillion (10^{12}).].

2   Fred Goldstein, "*Capitalism at a Dead-End: Job Destruction, Overproduction and Crisis in the High Tech Era: A Marxist View*," *Workers World*, 11 June 2011, accessed 21 July 2014, http://www.workers.org/ebooks/CapitalismDeadEnd.pdf.

On the other hand, the structural crisis unfolding in the centre of the global capitalist system has affected (and will increasingly affect) the main economies and societies of the world whether in Latin America, Africa and Asia, or the European Union. In so far as the measures taken by the US government to date (as well as by European countries) are financial in nature, we can infer that for capital and large corporations there is no way forward other than to deposit the entire weight of the crisis on the shoulders of workers and society. This will be felt in the form of cuts to wages, massive dismissals from companies in both the manufacturing and service sectors, cuts to social services, reductions in the value of pensions and increases to the age of retirement, all of which will be accompanied by a clear increase in the rate of exploitation through longer working days, greater intensity in the labour process and increasingly, through reductions to the consumption fund of workers as a portion is converted into an additional source of capital. This last measure will take place with the clear objective of increasing corporate profits, particularly those of the most powerful firms or, in other words, monopolies with an enormous capacity for international management.

Only a few months earlier, no sane person would have thought that such a situation could arise in a country that had successfully transformed itself into the global hegemon following the Second World War; just as, similarly, few foresaw the collapse of the Soviet Union in the nineteen-nineties, which had previously been identified as the beachhead of actually existing socialism. From that moment, it was thought that with the absence of this superpower, the United States would remain the unilateral power able to command in the service of all imperialist interests around the globe. Today, to the contrary, if it is still capable of maintaining its status as an above-all military power, the United States increasingly appears to suffer economic, social and political weaknesses, as well as setbacks within the shifting geostrategic map of the great powers and the arrival of so-called emerging powers led by China.

This crisis has also been reflected in the sphere of thought and ideology. To the extent that its main currents are framed by dominant thinking and within the epistemological spaces tolerated by capitalism, they have also proven limited in their ability to analyse and assess structural problems stemming from the crisis and the constant systemic imbalances in economic, social, political and cultural terms. It is in this sense that the majority of theoretical expressions (or paradigms formed in previous decades) have been immersed in a universe characterised by vagueness and uncertainty in terms of their depth of analysis, in relation to both the structural crisis of capitalism, and to future prospects open to workers and humanity. Scholars of social science committed to the existing order, in particular, have systematically evaded this issue. At its root, this 'epistemic' conjuncture should be understood as the product of the intense over-determination and hegemony of dominant ideas grounded in capitalist market ideology and individualistic egocentrism as the engines of human history and society.

The view in the first decade of the 21st century is tremendously unsettling: the social sciences and their associated schools of thought are, for all intents and purposes, confounded with neoliberal discourses focussed on the free market, extreme methodological individualism, and with crude social Darwinism. They have proven incapable of formulating hypotheses and assessments to frame autonomous and objective research that genuinely reflects the essence of the phenomena under study *without* the interference of eurocentric paradigms and those filtered through with the positivist and racist content of dominant ideologies. The latter have taken the baton, setting the agenda for academic investigation and content by using the political power they exercise in the media and systems of student funding, financing institutions of higher and post-graduate education, and creating and collaborating with institutes and research centres oriented towards neoliberal interests. For this reason it is urgent to recover the autonomy and critical capacity of Latin American thought to allow it to create its own epistemologies, theoretical frameworks and research methods; an effort leading to the development of *its own* categories and concepts which are a true reflection of the *essential* metabolism of social and human phenomena extending throughout the world in the early 21st century.

In this setting, if it is true that historical and dialectical materialism suffered one of its greatest setbacks towards the end of the 80s with the ideological effects of the disintegration of the USSR and the rise of neoliberal ideology with the Washington Consensus, it also began to re-emerge following the structural crisis of capital and its dominant ideologies as the main paradigm and current of 21st century critical and revolutionary thought. Historical and dialectical materialism re-emerged as a means to account for the essence of the crisis and to develop ways of overcoming it by creating new spaces of reflection and analysis to support the construction of a new alternative to capitalist society, its modes of production and consumption based on private property and the market, and the exploitation of the workforce in service of the production of surplus value and profit.

In this context, we understand the historical crisis of the capitalist mode of production and of labour to be the product of the increasing macro- and micro-economic difficulties faced by capital in the production of value and surplus value which are systematically being 'resolved' by, in fact, *deepening* the tendency of the rate of profit to fall and the fundamental contradictions of the system. For capital to be distributed and consumed in society it must first be produced; hence, the act of production is the axis around which the entire dynamic of capitalist reproduction and labour power turns. Thus, when production is interrupted the system goes into crisis and is thrown into arduous contradictions that can be resolved at times, and at other times not. Over the long run, state policies (predominantly monetary and financial) prove to be insufficient and even counterproductive in the effort to counteract the crisis without creating new contradictions and difficulties that become intractable over time. In this sense, the housing or financial crises that have emerged in advanced capitalist countries and, in the era of globalised capital, branched off into dependent and underdeveloped countries have structural roots, and have found new life in the field of the production of value and capital valorisation to affect the spheres of circulation and national and global markets.

The crisis of capital is a wide-ranging phenomenon that nonetheless manifests more or less sharply at specific conjunctures. In this sense, prolonged recessions have appeared in the global economy, as opposed to episodic declines in growth and development: systemic crises to the detriment of structural stability; processes associated with the 'fracturing' of globalisation due to the emergence of neo-protectionist and neo-Keynesian practices; the power of transnational corporations and their ties to hegemonic, imperialist States capable of influencing national cycles of capital; the recessive pressures of speculative activities (or fictitious capital, in Marx's terminology) on productive systems; and the decline in the production of value, surplus value and thus, in the rate of profit, which is being used to rationalise the effort (or intention) of capital to universalise methods of exploitation and of extracting absolute and relative surplus value under the logic of recovering the rate of profit. In this context, it has become necessary to put in place those methods of organizing production and labour exploitation (such as Toyotism and flexible automation) that have been applied to modern productive processes within major transnational companies at work in both developed and dependent countries. Understanding the roots of the crisis should be a fundamental task of workers and their organisations, to orient their struggles beyond mere, albeit legitimate, material demands (salaries, benefits, social welfare) towards the construction of a new economic and social system, based on non-alienated labour and the (re)integration of the interests and demands of the great mass of working humanity.

The present work is divided into two parts. Part I seeks to locate the intrinsic connection between the crisis of capital and the ways in which abstract labour determines value and surplus value by examining two further issues: first, the issue of the *dismeasure of value* and, second, the crisis understood in terms of a crisis of value and surplus value production that has facilitated the deviation of capital reproduction towards the unproductive, speculative spheres of fictitious capital. This, in turn, has generated pressure on the productive sphere to contract in scale and spurred the restructuring of labour processes to adjust them to capital's dynamic of concentration and valorisation; over the medium term, this will see the deterioration of employment, salaries and qualifications. To support our hypothesis, Chapter 1 examines the centrality of labour as an economic, ontological and political category as well as the multiple instances of its antipode to capital. Chapter 2 returns to the concepts of constant and variable capital and their relation to the labour process so as to recuperate the contention that only labour power is capable of simultaneously reproducing its own value and creating a new one (surplus labour) that takes the form of surplus value. Finally, Chapter 3 deals with abstract labour with the help of categories found in the *Grundrisse* and *Capital* such as the dismeasure of value, which, in our view, presupposes that the category of 'socially-necessary labour time' has become inadequate for the extraction of surplus value. As such, capital has had to maximise surplus value extraction in order to restore the conditions for its own reproduction and to elevate rates of profit throughout the system.

Part II of the present work examines a tendency to generalise the super-exploitation of labour as a category that can be seen throughout the system. While super-exploitation continues to determine the character of dependent capitalism, economic, political and ideological pressure have also seen it extended to the economic and productive systems of advanced capitalism. In this regard, Chapter 4 addresses the relationship between surplus value and labour super-exploitation in the labour theory of value, particularly the contributions of Ruy Mauro Marini to the sociology of labour in this regard. We consider the debate surrounding the existence of a world characterised by two patterns of capital accumulation: the dominant mode based on relative surplus value and the productivity of labour and, second, capital accumulation at work in dependent economies based on the greater exploitation of the worker. Finally, we turn to the hypothesis that in today's world, on the cusp of the future of work in the 21st century, labour power has become the strategic factor in the production of extraordinary profits thereby contradicting the thesis of the end of work.

Chapter 5 highlights some elements of the new morphology of capitalism in which the countries of the former socialist bloc have been converted into true *peripheries* of the hegemonic countries of advanced capitalism (Germany, France, England and Italy). These countries play various role including, among others, as sources of pressure to lower the wages of workers in central countries, to increase the rates of labour exploitation, and to serve as platforms for capital accumulation and reproduction for the transnational corporations of hegemonic countries. Here the focus of the discussion (and our working hypothesis) is that while the super-exploitation of labour in dependent capitalism is a hegemonic category that subordinates relative surplus value (along with other archaic forms of exploitation and production), in advanced capitalism it primarily governs the reproduction of capital and even over-determines the constitution and concrete forms that super-exploitation takes in the context of its historical and structural specificities. Finally, we draw to an end with this debate and conclude that there is a clear tendency towards greater rates of exploitation in advanced countries, as indicated by current neoliberal policies of social austerity which are aimed at deconstructing the welfare state that emerged following the Second World War.

PART 1

Structural Crisis and Abstract Labour

∵

CHAPTER 1

Capital-labour as Antipodes?

> The *devaluation* of the human world
> grows in direct proportion to
> the *increase in value* of the world of things.
> Labor not only produces commodities;
> it also produces itself and
> the workers as a commodity and
> it does so in the same proportion
> in which it produces commodities in general.
> KARL MARX, *Economic and Philosophical Manuscripts of 1844*[1]

Introduction

There is no doubt that over the last three decades a series of sudden trans-formations has changed the profile of contemporary societies and productive processes globally from what they were during the first half of the 20th century. Economies have become more tightly interlinked through so-called globalisation. Class structures have become more hierarchical, incorporating new sectors and classes in processes of change that shape their specific demands alongside those of traditional worker and proletarian movements which have been seriously hit, de-structured and restructured by State economic policy and repression, as well as by the mercantilist activities of big capital that adopted neoliberalism as its strategic policy.

Significant transformations in the structure of the State and political power have required the adoption of new theories and approaches capable of explaining them. The general juridical and formal democratisation of political regimes that took place over the course of the eighties was particularly noteworthy in this sense, particularly in Latin America, beginning with the removal of the dictatorial regimes that had established counterinsurgency States based on repressive force and military power that were hegemonic during the sixties and seventies. Also of great importance was the disintegration of the Soviet Union and Soviet bloc in so far as it changed the international map by adding

---

1 Karl Marx, "Economic and Philosophical Manuscripts (1844)," in *Marx Early Writings*, translated by Rodney Livingstone and Gregor Benton, 279–400 (London: Penguin, 1975).

a new geopolitical dimension to American unilateralism which would allow it to conduct new interventions and aggressions with impunity (such as the Gulf War against Iraq), as well as leading to the subsequent breakdown of US hegemony with the rise of new regional powers like China, India, Iran and Pakistan.

All of these factors have taken a toll on the main paradigms of social thought to differing degrees and at different levels and, in our view, have impeded their ability to fulfil their substantive task: to deeply analyse whether these interlinked historical changes have transformed the essence of the capitalist system as a whole or, as we believe (while certainly profound) they have simply changed the *form* of certain dimensions of the system and contemporary society.

In this chapter, our aim is to examine trends in the world of work that have altered its profile over this period, ostensibly generating a *new morphology of labour*. This has been expressed in new forms of capital accumulation and valorisation: in worker and professional categories and in novel forms of remuneration for salaried work, in structural transformations that have expanded the scope of the traditional factory, turning society itself into a 'social factory' and, finally, in the rise of a *new organisation of labour* which has broken with and rearticulated the old rhythm of mass production of Fordism-Taylorism, to become refined in new paradigms such as the Japanese Toyotism system and flexible automation, two structural components of the new forms of *being* of labour and capital.

The above can be reduced to the question of whether *labour* (in a framework that presupposes the centrality of capital as an antagonistic subject, which no-one disputes) continues to be a *central category* in the new economic, social and political capitalist order, or whether it has now been 'superseded' in favour of new forms of technology, science, information and communication, as some authors and schools of social thought have posited in an effort to explain the current order.

The World of Work: Extinction or Centrality in the Current Day?

The dominant ideology has imposed a system of ideas that has succeeded in convincing the majority of humanity of the 'values and virtues' of capitalism, understood to be an eternal and omnipresent system. To this end, it has developed what can be called 'axiomatic filters' that ultimately inform global public opinion. In general, these include:

1.   The market is the only instrument capable of solving the problems arising from human existence.

2.   Liberal democracy is the only 'perfect' system.

3.   Globalisation and competition are 'creative' realities that, while perfectible, cannot be turned back.

4.   The global market is comprised of fair relations of exchange and equilibrium between nations, where all are 'equals.'

5.   Human freedom is guaranteed by economic and political freedom.[2]

Amongst many other fashionable matters that mainstream thinking has placed on the agenda in applying these filters, we draw attention to the alleged 'displacement and extinction of labour' and consequently, of all the categories associated with its existence: value, surplus value, its salaried character, the conditions of its exploitation in society and, above all, its condition of being the only 'factor' of production capable of generating a value above its own. In the context of this authentically animistic notion, it has been declared that there are 'other' factors and determinants in contemporary society that now play this role such as technology, communications and, above all, immaterial labour. Authors of Marxist origin have taken the latter to task for ripping up the labour theory of value in order to 'prove' that there are other factors in (capitalist?) society responsible for the creation of commodities and wealth. Hence, the 'need' to create (or bring together theories of the 'end of work') a new social theory that attends to these 'new' phenomena derived from post-modernity and post-industrial society.

We should clarify that we do not deny the necessity of constructing new concepts and categories to account for all of these changes taking place in the social order. However, this is far from a call to create a 'new social theory' in so far as the first thing that needs to be fully discussed is whether these trends have truly changed the essence of the economic system founded on the capitalist mode of production, or whether they only affect the manner in which it currently functions and manifests. At any rate, it is more productive and indeed crucial to develop an understanding of the changes in course and to construct an *expanded conception of labour*. At best it should be accepted that a major change has come about in the capitalist system; as Sennett writes: "The indifference of the old class-based capitalism was starkly material; the indifference which radiates out of flexible capitalism is more personal because the system itself is less starkly etched, less legible in form."[3]

---

2   Armando Fernández Steinko, *Clase, trabajo y ciudadanía. Introducción a la existencia social* (Madrid: Biblioteca Nueva, 2004), 32.

3   Richard Sennett, *The Corrosion of Character: The Personal Consequences of Work in the New Capitalism* (London: W.W. Norton & Co., 1998), 146.

This apologetic *bricolage* related to the presumed 'extinction' of work appeared as the 'knowledge society' which had supposedly left behind (and surpassed) advanced industrial and mass society which, in turn, had been sustained by the industrial production of material goods and services by salaried (alienated) work and by capital accumulation. Where the latter context produced two 'paradigms' in the theory of social systems (capitalism and socialism, both with their respective modes of production, types of society and institutional state apparatuses), the former has produced theories of post-industrial society based on the predominance of financial services, technology and science. These are represented by various authors including Raymond Aron, Alain Touraine, John Kenneth Galbraith, Herbert Marcuse and Daniel Bell as well as in three main streams of systemic-positivist theory: (1) the knowledge society of Peter Drucker, Daniel Bell, and Nico Stehr; (2) the theory of the information society of Manuel Castells and his 'network society' during the 1990s; and (3), the 'communication society' of Jürgen Habermas.[4] Nonetheless,

> The end of the 20th century and the first decade of the 21st proved false the predications of those who imagined a post-industrial, post-capitalist and post-modern world in which labour would lose both its ontological significance in the configuration of human beings, as its significance in support of the emancipation of humanity, and even its fundamental role in the extraction of surplus value and the reproduction of capital.[5]

These approaches undermine the conception of the labour-capital *antipode* as the strategic focus of class struggle and of social conflict more generally— much less as the *motor* of history—in so far as they attempt to displace and relegate it in favour of new forces, determinants, relations and conceptions led by the forces of technology, the market, communication and, even more so, by the 'objective' actions of the State through public policies which shape and even overdetermine social endeavours. Thus they argue that institutions such

---

4   Peter Drucker, *The Age of Discontinuity* (New York: Harper & Row, 1969); Daniel Bell, *The Coming of Post-industrial Society: A Venture in Social Forecasting* (New York: Basic Books, 1973); Nico Stehr, *Knowledge Societies* (Thousand Oaks, California: Sage Publications, 1994); Manuel Castells, *The Information Age: Economy, Society and Culture. Volume I: The Rise of the Network Society* – 2nd edition (Oxford: Blackwell, 2002); Jürgen Habermas, *The Theory of Communicative Action. Volume 2: Lifeworld and System; a Critique of Functionalist Reason* (Boston: Beacon Press, 1989).

5   Virginia Fontes, *O capital-imperialismo* (Rio de Janeiro: Editora UFRJ, 2010), 150.

as the school and university have become the centre of social protest against the economic and political apparatuses of the State. 'New subjects' such as students, researchers, young people, teachers or experts and professionals who exercise roles of responsibility will be the drivers of contemporary revolutionary movements. The working class, on the other hand, the former historical subject of this struggle and of Marx's labour theory of value itself, has ceased to be a privileged social actor or (similar to the employer) the key element of the system of power and of transformation in the post-industrial society!

Dos Santos, for example, assumes this position when he maintains that, over the last 30 years, it has been the Indigenous, peasants, women, Afrodescendents, *piqueteros* and the unemployed who have driven the 'most advanced' social struggles, although he does not specify what kind of achievements they have produced or the content of their objectives. And this serves as a foundation from which to suggest that "the modern solutions proposed by liberalism and also by Marxism no longer work, even if pushed to their maximum possible consciousness...."[6] At a theoretical level, this statement is clearly unsustainable given that it does not consider the reasons why Marxism is supposedly no longer capable of providing 'solutions' (left undefined), nor what constitutes Marxism in the 21st century. Secondly, it elides the issue of whether social classes continue to exist in the contemporary world and if so, what they are. Finally, it neglects the problem of the subject, of consciousness and of the real possibilities of transcending the current system, and of giving birth to a human, economic, social and political system superior to capitalism.

Faced with these conservative conceptions which have ultimately transformed knowledge of capitalist society into a true theoretical pandemonium, a critical paradigm arose represented by three currents: (a) the labour theory of value that returns to Marx (particularly the *Grundrisse* and *Capital*); (b) Antonio Gramsci, György Lukács (*Urphänomen*) and other contemporary Marxist authors such as István Mészáros; the Italian School of the 'general intellect,' including Antonio Negri and Maurício Lazzarato with the concept of 'immaterial labour'; and (c) critical postures within Marxism, such as that of Ricardo Antunes, Giovanni Alves, and this author who all maintain the continuing *centrality of labour* in contemporary capitalist society and who recognise immaterial labour *within* the material cycle of labour and the production

---

6 Boaventura de Sousa Santos, "Public Sphere and Epistemologies of the South," *Africa Development* 37(1) (2012): 46 [Spanish quotation taken from Boaventura de Sousa Santos, *Refundación del Estado en América Latina. Perspectivas desde una epistemología del sur* (Ciudad de México: Universidad de los Andes, Siglo del Hombre Editores, Siglo XXI Editores, 2010), 39.].

process and, therefore, within Marx's labour theory of value.[7] Alves, for example, writes:

> The tendency towards the 'suppression' [of labour in the capital 'subject'], never feasible within the logic of the valorisation of 'living labour', does not negate the ontological centrality of the category of labour (that is, the centrality of the signifier 'labour' as maintained by Habermas, Offe and Gorz) since what tends to emerge, once again, is the capital 'subject' as 'dead labour'. In this sense, labour tends to arise with the emergence of the 'capital subject' as a negated premise in the logical (and ontological) sense; that is, as alienated, protracted and universal labour.[8]

Antunes, in turn, reveals that:

> ...governed by the destructiveness of capital and the market, it was the very form that the *society of work* took, with a mass of workers thrown out of the productive process, that made the *appearance* of a society founded on the *decentring* of the category of labour and the loss of the centrality of work in the contemporary world possible. But the understanding of the changes in progress, such as the development of a *broader notion of work*, has become essential to understanding the *form of being of labour* in the contemporary world, its new morphology, and its *multifaceted character*.[9]

Further along, the author defines his *broadened* conception of labour, with which we agree. He writes:

> To understand the new form of being of labour it is necessary to begin from a broader conception of work, which out of necessity considers the totality of the working class: the enormous contingent of men and women living today from the sale of their labour power, and not only directly manual workers. This conception should also incorporate the totality of social labour, the totality of collective labour that sells its labour-power as a commodity in exchange for a wage; however, the enormous excess contingent of the workforce that does not find work, due to

---

7 Ricardo Antunes, *Los sentidos del trabajo* (Buenos Aires. Ediciones Herramienta, 2005); Giovanni Alves, *A condição da proletariedade* (Londrina, São Paulo: Editora Praxis, 2009).

8 Alves, *A condição*, 59.

9 Antunes, *Los sentidos*, 239.

the destructive logic which commands capitalist society, should also be included.[10]

Those authors who follow in the footprint of the *general intellect* school of thought maintain that the cycle of immaterial labour can be described as follows: (a) 'work' has become 'immaterial,' the workforce a 'mass intellect' that produces subjectivity and knowledge, and immaterial labour hegemonic in society; (b) in this context, manual labour no longer carries the same weight in the production of goods and services and is in steady decline; and conversely, (c) intellectual labour has emerged and become generalised; (d) intellectual work has consequently become equated with knowledge; and, (e) the activity of 'immaterial workers' can be found in advertising, fashion, marketing, the entertainment industries, finance, information and communications, and computer programming (software).

Lazzarato, for example, illustrates what is for him the *specificity* of immaterial labour with respect to 'traditional' forms of capital reproduction while also maintaining that this work 'possesses' its 'own, autonomous cycle.'

1. 'Productive synergies' are autonomous since 'immaterial labour' is a superior synthesis of varying kinds of *savoir-faire*, namely, intellectual, manual, and entrepreneurial activities. According to the author, the nature of the activities of immaterial labour "forces us to re-examine the classical definitions of 'work' and 'workforce'."[11]
2. The 'ideological product' becomes a commodity but does not lose its autonomy. At the same time, it "produces new stratifications of reality," which is the result of the increasing "power of knowledge and human action." "New modes of being and feeling" are created which require new technologies which, in turn, require new modes of being and feeling.[12]

10   Ricardo Antunes, *O continente do labor* (São Paulo: Boitempo Editorial, 2011), 49.
11   Maurizio Lazzarato, "Immaterial Labour," trans. Paul Colilli and Ed Emery, *The Generation-Online Blog*, accessed 15 May 2014, http://www.generation-online.org/c/fcimmateriallabour3.htm.
12   Ideology is not the same thing as knowledge. While it is true that the former shapes the latter, in the world of commodities, knowledge is appropriated by capital for production, while ideology is the idiographic expression of the forms of domination of capital that resounds in both the fetishisation of society as well as the strengthening of the capitalist system as the producer of goods, including the workforce that produces and reproduces it as such.

3.   The "public" (which is left undefined) possesses a "double productive
     function": on the one hand, it is a "constitutive element of 'work'" and, on
     the other, it is part of "social communication."

4.   The recreation of the product as the "commodity" does not eliminate "the
     open process of creation that is established between immaterial labour
     and the public, and which is organized through communication." As we
     can see, it is the latter and not the process of material production that
     sees the 'integration' of the public (consumer) in immaterial labour. This
     point resonates with Habermas's thesis when it suggests that, in contrast
     to the "world of work" which remains part of the system (in other words,
     of the systemic structure of technical, bureaucratic, institutional ration-
     ality), there is "communicative action" which belongs to the "world of
     life" and of "subjects" with the capacity for transformation.[13]

Critical thought diverges from these ideological positions and holds that: (a)
material labour organises manual and intellectual labour; (b) knowledge is
essential to the material production of goods and services; (c) *without* labour
in general, it is not possible to understand the current form of global capitalist
society, production and life; and (d) labour is central to the new (precarious,
part time, domestic, outsourced, informal) dimensions introduced by productive restructuring (the new *morphology* of labour). But the central point here is
that abstract labour (which is in systemic crisis) has not changed since the
historical foundations of capitalism. What we have seen, rather, are abrupt and
contradictory changes that have altered its *morphology*, its concrete forms, its
multiple determinations:

> ...it was the very form taken by the *society of work*, governed by the destruc-
> tiveness of capital and the market, which, with a mass of workers thrown
> out of the productive process, made possible the appearance of a society
> founded on the *decentring* of the category of labour, the loss of the centrality
> of work in the contemporary world. But understanding the changes in
> progress, both the development of *a broadened conception of work*, became
> essential to understanding *the form of being that labour* takes in the contem-
> porary world, its new morphology, as well as its *multifaceted character*.[14]

---

13   Jürgen Habermas, *The Theory of Communicative Action. Volume 2: Lifeworld and System:
     A Critique of Functionalist Reason* (Boston: Beacon Press, 1989), 113 *et seq.*

14   Antunes, *Los sentidos*, 239. Marx argues that the nature of capital is essentially the same
     whether it appears in its more or less developed forms, and this should be central to any
     theoretical reflection on the contemporary world of work by critical thought.

Authors critical of the 'end of labour' thesis correctly observe a conceptual and theoretical misconception regarding concrete labour (use value) and abstract labour (exchange value) both in the conservative and the *general intellect* schools of thought; while the former has undergone qualitative and quantitative changes (flexibilisation, precarisation), the latter is responsible for the production of surplus value in general and has remained central to the reproduction of the system, despite undergoing the periodic crises we see today. As Antunes concludes:

> The misunderstanding and disregard for this *double and decisive dimension* of labour has led many authors to mistake the social crisis of *abstract labour* for a social crisis of *concrete labour*. And from there, to mistakenly defend the notion of the end of labour.[15]

We are reminded of this statement from Shaik: "Capitalism's sheath mutates constantly in order for its core to remain the same."[16]

Why Speak of Antipodes?

The existence of labour and capital as antipodes in capitalist society is neither a quirk nor an unspeakable fatality, much less an illusion conjured by outdated intellectuals. It is rather a daily reality that feeds the metabolic necessities of capitalist society, which is structured by social class and governed by the constitutive principle of private property. As much as its morphology has gone through obvious changes beginning in the last quarter of the 20th century, as we have suggested, abstract labour cannot disappear. In fact, these changes have been expressed in increasingly complex and divergent social relations, as well as in accelerated urbanisation and the rise of new areas of capital valorisation (new technologies, fictitious capital) such as telecommunications, information technologies, telematics, microelectronics, marketing and post-taylorist forms of labour organisation such as Toyotism, connected to processes of capital production and valorisation.

Social capital on a global scale, with its network of apparatuses and institutions, is thus shown to be the product of (dead, prior) labour whose reproduc-

---

15   Ricardo Antunes, "La dialéctica entre el trabajo concreto y el trabajo abstracto," *Revista Herramienta* (Buenos Aires) 44 (2010), 43, accessed 9 June 2014, http://www.herramienta.com .ar/revista-herramienta-n-44/la-dialectica-entre-el-trabajo-concreto-y-el-trabajo-abstracto.

16   Anwar Shaikh, "The First Great Depression of the 21st Century," *Socialist Register* 47 (2011): 46.

tion and preservation relies on living labour, regardless of the form it takes. Here, rather than being the 'individual worker' at play, or the 'concrete worker' (miner, mason, metalworker, technician or programmer) and the particular activity that he or she performs (to produce so much *use value*), it is the *global collective worker* that organises and articulates the productive and unproductive workers in society that are necessary to the self-valorisation of capital, in the aim of producing surplus value and increasing the rate of profit.

In summary, what we see is less the struggle between the individual worker and individual capital than one between the global, collective worker and social capital as a representative of the total interests of its class.

Why does It Persist in the 21st Century?

There are many factors that explain why the struggle between labour and capital still continues in a society thrown into chaos by structural and systemic crisis, by intense social and political struggles and serious fissures in the system of domination. We can cite the following:

1. Labour is the living substance of capital; it constitutes its use value without which capitalist production would collapse;
2. Without abstract labour, goods would lack the substance of exchange value, even though their use value (being enough to satisfy human need) would remain;
3. In such a context, only use value would continue to exist, implying the disappearance of abstract labour, and mercantile exchange (the quintessential motor of capitalist society) would cease;
4. Science and technology, while reifying prior and dead labour, would only maintain the production of wealth on a temporary basis, while transferring their (prior) value to commodity-production produced 'without the participation of labour.'

But there is a more profound issue that prevents the self-valorisation of capital without the participation of workers as a collective workforce. In today's world, as Mészáros suggests,

Under the changed circumstances some of the most powerful instruments of mystification—through which capital managed to exercise its paralysing ideological control over labour in the past—become dangerously undermined and tend to collapse altogether. For now the immense tensions generated within the system of capital production cannot be exported on an adequately massive scale at the expense of other countries, and thus, the basic social antagonism between capital and labour which lies at the roots of such tensions cannot be sealed down indefinitely: *the contradictions must be fought out at the place where they are actually generated.*[17]

Thus, "the real nature of the capitalist production relations: the ruthless domination of labour by capital is becoming increasingly more evident as a *global* phenomenon."[18] Moreover, there is a contradictory relationship between labour and capital which makes modern society inconceivable without the permanent antagonism of the two. And so,

> while capital's dependency on labor is *absolute*—in that capital is absolutely nothing without labour, which it must permanently exploit—labor's dependency on capital is *relative, historically created and historically surmountable*. In other words, labor is not condemned by remain permanently locked into capital's vicious cycle.[19]

In certain periods, the *subjects* of the world of labour are kept alienated by the force of capital's (ideological, administrative, cultural, political, juridical, repressive—all combined) instruments of class domination. Moreover, they frequently project a distorted 'media projection' that some sociological currents have interpreted as signalling the 'decline' of the 'revolutionary subject.' In a sense, this is a valid effort by some to understand this reality and its cause(s):

> Class consciousness is much more typical of the dominant classes, while competition, fragmentation, individualisation and division tend to be the norm amongst the fractions of the subaltern classes.[20]

---

17   István Mészáros, *Beyond Capital: Towards a Theory of Transition* (New York: Monthly Review, 1995), 890.

18   Ibid.

19   István Mészáros, *Socialism or Barbarism: From the "American Century" to the Crossroads* (New York: Monthly Review, 2001), 76–77 (italics in the original) [Spanish quotation taken from Mészáros, *Más allá del capital. Hacia una teoría de la transición* (Caracas: Vadell Hermanos Editores, 2001), XXXVII.].

20   Klause Dorre, in Fernández, *Clase,* 60.

But despite the unfavourable situation of the working and exploited classes, they are not content to exist, and to remain, in the antipode created by capital, as clearly expressed by the mass struggles of workers of Europe today following the deep systemic and structural crisis of capitalism; and in various nations of the Middle East and North Africa where workers and populations have taken to the streets in their struggle for better living and working conditions, and in their bid to overthrow the dictatorial governments of countries like Tunisia, Egypt and others, with an insurrectional stance.

Conclusion

As the central antipode of contemporary society, the labour-capital relation is a reality that is nourished daily by the social metabolism of capital and class society. The very existence of capital is empirical proof of the significance of labour, to the extent that the former is a crystallisation of accumulated labour. While technology, science, information and communications (supposedly at the heart of how 'post-industrial societies' function) are very important elements of human society and contribute greatly to the valorisation of capital, these processes should be understood as being organised in close interaction with labour, as producer both of value and surplus value. For without labour or value, it is impossible to understand society today.

As such, labour remains a central and valid category, not only in the context of the production of value but also in the social and political context, regardless of the transformations that the class structure (in particular, the proletariat and working class) has seen in recent years. In this same sense, it is necessary to understand the new morphology of labour and its role in social struggles at the national, regional and global levels and, also, how it articulates with the struggles and movements of other social and popular classes and movements which are claiming their rights and interests within the existing order.

The Labour Process and Productive Labour in Contemporary Capitalism

Introduction

In this chapter it is necessary to reflect on Marx's *Capital* for the purpose of dispelling and clarifying certain points of confusion related to the labour theory of value, which is essential for comprehending the current crisis of capital and its significance. To this end, it is crucial to remember the nature of the labour process realised by labour power, its instruments of production, and the object upon which the human activity of labour take place (i.e., nature). Here we discover that, contrary to all appearances and out of all of these factors, it is labour power alone that has the capacity to create a value equal to itself and, at the same time, to produce new value during production which is the surplus value that the capitalist expropriates.

At a later point, this thesis will serve to ground the argument that labour is a strategic category both for securing extraordinary profits and to maintain societies based on the capitalist mode of production.

The Labour Process (Constant and Variable Capital): A Re-evaluation

The labour theory of value proposes that the value of commodities is determined by the labour time that is socially necessary to produce them. Marini writes,

> ...socially-necessary labour time is not determined by the *circulation* of labour power but is rather the exclusive function of the development of productive forces, the degree of skill, productivity and average intensity of labour power in the context of production. The only thing that falls to circulation is the task of *comparing* socially-necessary labour times in the production of commodities; in other words, to compare their values. On this basis, the market price of each one is determined (i.e., a *price relation* between them is established) which, while varying in

response to supply and/or demand, *revolves around the comparison of values*.[1]

The *quantity* of labour is expressed in units of *time* (an hour, ten hours, etc.) and its price ultimately in units of money.[2] This mode of determining the value of a commodity value operates in any commerce-based society founded upon private ownership over the means of production and consumption, as well as exploitation and domination over the salaried workforce by capital.[3]

One cannot have an objective and dialectical view of the labour theory of value if its theoretical unity is not kept in mind. This unity speaks to the reproduction of capital in bourgeois society[4] and, in methodological terms, corresponds to the overall structure of *Capital*: volume I which examines the production process, volume II which deals with circulation, and volume III which focuses on the process of reproduction *as a whole*. Marx broaches the analysis of capital production itself beginning in the third part of volume I ("The Production of Absolute Surplus Value") and particularly in Chapter VI ("The Labour-Process and the Process of Producing Surplus-Value"). Here he sets out the scientific foundation for the analysis of the production of value

---

1 Ruy Mauro Marini, "Las razones del neodesarrollismo" (respuesta a Fernando Enrique Cardoso y José Serra)," *Revista Mexicana de Sociología* (Ciudad de México) XL (1978): 64.

2 "A use-value, or useful article, therefore, has value only because human labour in the abstract has been embodied or materialised in it. How, then, is the magnitude of this value to be measured? Plainly, by the quantity of the value-creating substance, the labour, contained in the article. The quantity of labour, however, is measured by its duration, and labour-time in its turn finds its standard in weeks, days, and hours." Karl Marx, *Capital – Volume I* (New York: International Publishers, 1974), 38.

3 Adrián Sotelo Valencia, *A reestruturação do mundo do trabalho. Superexploração e novos paradigmas de organização do trabalho* (Minas Gerais: Editora da Universidade Federal de Uberlândia, 2009), 41–42.

4 We believe it an enormous mistake to overlook the dialectical unity of Marx's *Capital* as Sergio Lessa has done in his book, *Trabalho e proletariado no capitalism contemporâneo* (São Paulo: Cortez Editora, 2007), when he writes that, "as volume I was the only one published by Marx, it should be the main reference point for the reading and interpretation of the remaining texts [i.e., volumes II and III]...," since for him, "...the final version [of volume I] came directly from its author" (25). If this were so, theoretical developments such as the more than 400-page long work of Rosa Luxemburg, *The Accumulation of Capital*, would be absolutely useless, in so far as its objects of study and debate are framed precisely by the concerns of volume II of *Capital*. In fact the work revitalises the idea of the dialectical articulation between production and circulation, the subject of the first two volumes. For an appreciative treatment, see Severo Salles, *Carlos Marx y Rosa Luxemburgo. La acumulación de capital en debate* (Buenos Aires: Peña Lillo, Ediciones Continente, 2009).

and surplus value. Marx devotes the two preceding sections to the problems of circulation (the commodity and the transformation of money into capital) as a *preamble*, before fully engaging the production of value and capital valorisation in the following two chapters. Important here is Marx's emphasis on the sphere of circulation where capital creates *neither* value *nor* surplus value. This idea is employed by certain authors of classical and neoclassical economics (as well as those working from a social democratic standpoint) in which value appears indiscriminately amongst all other 'factors of production' ('land,' 'capital,' 'technology,' 'science,' and even machinery or building structures used in production); ignoring the fact that, with the exception of the labour power that engenders them, the only action that these 'factors' perform is to transfer their prior value.

One example will be enough to illustrate the point. Disregarding the fact that labour is a commodity that is bought and sold on the market, and which is the object of trade, Dominique Méda maintains that labour is a 'collective act' and that wealth (sic) is,

> the product of a series of *complex interactions* in which capital, information systems, machines and human labour take part; interactions which signify that it is *no longer possible to maintain that human labour is the sole producer of wealth*. Today, human labour is so interwoven with a series of machines and systems that it makes it impossible to determine their exact contribution to the process.[5]

To follow this line of reasoning is to conclude that labour and labour power have ultimately evaporated and that in their place, value, surplus value and social wealth have become the work and provenance of negative value or, in a word, of divine spirit. This conception is very distant from the economic and social reality of capitalism which increasingly and *really* subsumes labour under its dominion in order to devour it, as well as being distant from the reality of societies kept at the 'margin' of capital's logic of production and exploitation. To the contrary, and as discussed earlier, labour power continues to be the essential and sole factor both in the production of the world's wealth and in the production of the value and surplus value that is appropriated by capital.

Returning to our exposition on the structure of *Capital*, in the third section of volume II Marx provides us with an overview of the reproduction of capital which he defines as the synthesis of the production process (labour process

---

5 Dominique Méda, *El trabajo. Un valor en extinción* (Barcelona: Gedisa, 1998), 146 (italics in the original).

and the production of surplus value, addressed in volume I) and the process of capital circulation which constitutes the *turnover of capital*:

> The direct process of the production of capital is its labour and self-expansion process, the process whose result is the commodity-product and whose compelling motive is the production of surplus-value. The process of reproduction of capital comprises this direct process of production as well as the two phases of the circulation process proper, i.e., the entire circuit which, as a periodic process—a process which constantly repeats itself in definite periods—constitutes the turnover of capital.[6]

In the *Grundrisse*, Marx had already pointed to the unity of capital that is necessary to guarantee its reproduction and, therefore, to begin the process of its production: "Capital, as production resting on wage labour, presupposes circulation as the necessary condition and moment of the entire motion."[7] Given these considerations, Marx distinguishes the *labour process* (lpr) and that of *value creation* as the process of producing commodities from the *process of valorising capital* (vc) as the specific form of capitalist commodity production. As it occurs in all social formations, the first is a universal characteristic and is comprised of three elements: (a) labour power (lp), (b) means of labour (ml), and (c) the object of labour (obj). The second process corresponds to valorisation involving only labour power and the new values it creates; the equivalent of the wage and surplus value (see Table 1). In Chapter VIII of the first volume of *Capital* ("Constant Capital and Variable Capital"), constant capital is created by the means of production (mp), machines, tools and raw materials.

TABLE 1   *The labour process and capital valorisation*

(1)	Labour process and value creation > process of production of commodities	
	(a) Labour power	> variable capital
	(b) Means of labour	
		> constant capital (mp)
	(c) Object of labour	
(2)	Valorisation process > form of producing commodities specific to capitalism	

---

6   Karl Marx, *Capital – Volume II* (New York: International Publishers, 1984), 355.

7   Karl Marx, *Grundrisse: Foundations of the Critique of Political Economy (Rough Draft)* (London: Penguin Books, 1993), 405–6.

That part of capital then, which is represented by the means of production, by the raw material, auxiliary material and the instruments of labour, does not, in the process of production, undergo any quantitative alteration of value. I therefore call it the constant part of capital or, more succinctly, *constant capital*. On the other hand, that part of capital, represented by labour-power does, in the process of production, undergo an alteration of value. It both reproduces the equivalent of its own value and also produces an excess, a surplus-value, which may itself vary and may be more or less according to circumstances. This part of capital is continually being transformed from a constant into a variable magnitude. I therefore call it the variable part of capital or, in more simplified terms, *variable capital*.[8]

Chapter VIII then examines how each one of the factors of the labour process (lp, ml, obj) affects the formation of the commodity's value ($C = c + v + sv$). The methodological procedure is as follows. Marx constructed the categories of variable capital and constant capital to illustrate that both new value and surplus value are produced *exclusively* by labour power rather than the means of production; and specifically, by its *useful* quality, or the use value that it possesses according to the law of value (i.e., by the quantity of socially-necessary labour time that went into its production and reproduction). In the same socially-necessary time and space the worker simultaneously (a) creates and replaces the value of his or her lp, (b) transfers prior dead labour contained in the mp to the new product or commodity, and (c) creates a new value in excess (surplus value) which the capitalist then appropriates as owner of the means of production and of the labour power (use) value. Marx pointed to the 'splitting' of the product during production into the part representing "only the labour previously spent on the means of production, or the constant capital, another only the variable capital, and another and last part, only the surplus-labour expended during the same process, or the surplus-value...."[9]

It is crucial to understand this last concept. The *dual character of labour* suggests that, when its productive activity is deployed in the labour process, the lp of the worker (a) conserves and transfers a value (of the mp, raw materials and instruments of labour), and (b) creates a *new* value that did not previously exist (i.e., a wage and surplus value). It is for this reason that Marx insisted that commodities contain both a use value and exchange value, and embody "this two-fold nature of the labour contained in commodities."[10] So important

---

8   Marx, *Capital – Volume I*, 209.

9   Ibid., 223.

10   Ibid., 41.

is this double character of labour that Marx himself considered it "...the pivot on which a clear comprehension of Political Economy turns."[11]

In this sense, Marx affirms the following: "The property therefore which labour-power in action, living labour, possesses of preserving value, at the same time that it adds it, is a gift of Nature";[12] and we would add, a gift which no other commodity (material or immaterial) possesses. This illustrates Marx's study of the role that the distinct parts of capital (labour power, means of production, instruments and object of labour) play in the valorisation process.

Theoretical Premises

As far as the mp, raw materials, and so on are concerned, they do not *create* value but rather transfer it to the finished product.[13] According to Aglietta, "...constant capital is a value transmitted to the value of the product during production."[14] As far as Marx is concerned, the:

> ...means of production never transfer more value to the product than they themselves lose during the labour-process by the destruction of their own use-value. If such an instrument has no value to lose, if, in other words, it is not the product of human labour, it transfers no value to the product. It helps to create use-value without contributing to the formation of exchange-value. In this class are included all means of production supplied by Nature without human assistance, such as land, wind, water, metals *in situ*, and timber in virgin forests.[15]

Once the value of the mp and of labour power (or the value equivalent to that which Marx calls *actual reproduction*) has been recovered by capital,[16] the remainder (sv¹) represents the valorisation of the original advanced capital (c + v). As the mp (raw materials, tools, etc.) do not create more value than they confer from past labour, Marx called them *constant capital*. And because labour power with its dual character (being producer of both use values and exchange values) *does* augment value when (a) it transfers and retains value,

11   Ibid.

12   Ibid., 206 (italics in the original).

13   Ibid., 205.

14   Michel Aglietta, *Regulación y crisis del capitalismo* (Madrid: Siglo XXI Editores, 1979), 36.

15   Marx, *Capital – Volume I*, 204.

16   Ibid., 208.

(b) it creates a value that is the equivalent of lp expended, and (c) it creates an excess or surplus value that otherwise would not exist, Marx called it *variable capital*.[17] This in fact provides sound theoretical grounding for the conception of workforce 'flexibility' which, rather than formally opposing it to 'rigidity', as neoclassical economic and functionalist sociology of labour have tended to do, combines them to obtain a dynamic and dialectical conception of the process of labour exploitation. One could say then that *variable capital*, or waged labour, is flexible from the start, while labour *flexiblisation* is the *realisation* and *adaptation* of its flexibility to the current conditions of capital accumulation. Currently, flexibility refers to the process of removing obstacles that hinder the free mobility of labour by capital, to make it possible to freely recruit and dismiss the workforce.[18]

The lpr and vc, then, constitute a unity of objective and subjective factors that are subsequently revealed in the concepts of constant capital and variable capital, as illustrated below in Table 2.

This framework reflects the necessary unity between manual and intellectual labour which are in no way independent of one another. Instead, they constitute a dialectical unity synthesised in labour power which is subsumed and exploited by capital.

One remaining issue relates to the question of whether changes to constant and variable capital following increased social productivity of labour do in fact modify the value of commodities. The conclusions that Marx reaches are striking: A *revolution* in constant capital *increases* the velocity of the *transference of value* but, *in and of itself, does not produce additional value*, an issue which ultimately tends to lower the rate of profit. If this factor actually increases the

TABLE 2   *The labour process and the process of valorisation*

Labour process		Valorisation process
Objective factors (*mp*)	→	Constant capital (c)
Subjective factors (*lp*)	→	Variable capital (v)
Value of C = c + v + sv		

---

17   Ibid., 209.

18   On the issue of flexibility and its definition, see Sennett, *Corrosion*. One institutional effort to confer a positive spin on flexibility is reflected in the concept of *flexicurity*. See Jürgen Weller, ed., *El Nuevo scenario laboral latinoamericano. Regulación, protección y políticas activas en los mercados de trabajo* (Buenos Aires: CEPAL, Siglo XXI Editores, 2009).

productivity of labour, without affecting its value, it generates extraordinary profit without adding value.[19]

On the issue of this relation of productivity to extraordinary profits, Marini put forward the following:

> ...to increase their productivity above the normal level that socially-necessary labour time has established...that is, above that which determines the social value of the commodity, the individual capitalist ensures that the same working day creates a greater production of value, simply because, despite the fact that the individual value of the commodity has fallen in real terms, it continues to hold the same social value; however, it is now produced in greater quantity. In short, given that value is a social relation, it is the social value which counts; the fact that the individual capitalist has reduced the unit value of his commodity is nothing but a way of saying that he has reduced his costs of production when compared to other capitalists in the branch. It is through this mechanism that the capitalist obtains an extraordinary surplus value, which is converted through inter-capitalist competition into the factor *par excellence* of introducing technological change.[20]

A revolution in variable capital (which improves the organisation of labour, making it more rational, efficient, flexible, versatile, competitive and profitable) *enhances* productivity (and therefore, the production of value) due to the rising exploitation of the workforce: the relation between socially-necessary labour time (nt) and unpaid surplus labour (st) on which the rate of surplus value (sv/v) depends.

In sum, only the ratio of the magnitude between constant and variable capital changes. Marx thus illustrates the scientific validity of the labour theory of value which posits that only labour power (or more precisely, the use value of the worker's labour power) can generate value and surplus value as determined by socially-necessary labour time (nt). In other words, and to paraphrase the happy expression of Mészáros, "capital is the parasite of labour" which it must exploit and dominate in order to survive. We should clarify that not just any work possesses this characteristic being able to generate surplus value. In other words, labour power must be productive with respect to capital valorisation in order to possess this property.

---

19   Marx, *Capital – Volume I*, Chapter VIII.

20   Ruy Mauro Marini, "Plusvalía extraordinaria y acumulación de capital," *Cuadernos Políticos* 20 (Ciudad de México) (April–June 1979): 24.

Productive and Unproductive Labour

In the theoretical structure of *Capital* the concepts of productive and unproductive labour play a central role in the interpretation of the theory of value and surplus value. Here, Marx suggests that "...the question whether capital is productive or not is absurd. Labour itself is *productive only* if absorbed into capital, where capital forms the basis of production, and where the capitalist is therefore in command of production";[21] as such, the capitalist does not create value nor surplus value *per se*, as neoclassical economics generally preaches. It is at this level of abstraction that the twin concepts of productive and unproductive labour are understood in relation to capital, to identify value-producing subjects—producers of social wealth, of surplus value and its (fetishised) derivative forms—accordingly, as well as the subject (or subjects) that directly or indirectly transform(s) nature with or without the benefit of technology. Moreover, they help to define the potentially *revolutionary subject* constituted by the force of social transformation by virtue of being the quintessential *antipode* of capital.

We begin with Chapter VII of the first volume of *Capital*, in which Marx defines productive labour thusly:

> If we examine the whole process from the point of view of its result, the product, it is plain that both the instruments and the subject of labour, are means of production, and that the labour itself is productive labour.

However, in the footnote, he adds:

> This method of determining, from the standpoint of the labour-process alone, what is productive labour, is by no means directly applicable to the case of the capitalist process of production.[22]

Returning to and resolving this conceptual (and consequently, analytical) limitation, in Chapter XVI, Marx explains "[t]hat labourer alone is productive, who produces surplus-value for the capitalist, and thus works for the self-expansion of capital."[23] And to permanently resolve this issue, he writes in the same chapter:

---

21   Marx, *Grundrisse*, 308.
22   Marx, *Capital – Volume I*, 181.
23   Marx, *Capital – Volume I*, 509.

As the co-operative character of the labour-process becomes more and more marked, so, as a necessary consequence, does our notion of productive labour, and of its agent the productive labourer, become extended. In order to labour productively, it is no longer necessary for you to do manual work yourself; enough, if you are an organ of the collective labourer, and perform one of its subordinate functions. The first definition given above of productive labour, a definition deduced from the very nature of the production of material objects, still remains correct for the collective labourer, considered as a whole. But it no longer holds good for each member taken individually.[24]

In this way, Marx *restricts* the concept of productive labour and its agent (the worker), in so far as capitalist production is no longer defined solely by commodity production (c + v + sv); it is rather fundamentally the production of surplus value (sv). At the same time as the concept of productive labour is restricted, it is also enriched by the combination of commodity production with that of surplus value; and at the same time, Marx insists that the (*collective*) worker no longer produces for him or herself but rather exclusively for capital, and is thus completely subordinated to it. This idea also figures in the unpublished version of Chapter VI which associates productive work with the real subsumption of the direct labour process by capital.[25]

In Chapter XVI of volume I we find a complement to both theses regarding productive and unproductive labour:

That labourer alone is productive, who produces surplus-value for the capitalist, and thus works for the self-expansion of capital. ...Hence the notion of a productive labourer implies not merely a relation between work and useful effect, between labourer and product of labour, but also a specific, social relation of production, a relation that has sprung up historically and stamps the labourer as the direct means of creating surplus-value.[26]

Marx confirms this definition in the following passage:

...with the development of the *real subsumption of labour under capital*, or the *specifically capitalist mode of production*, the *real lever* of the overall

---

24   Marx, *Capital – Volume I*, 508–9.
25   Karl Marx, "Results of the Immediate Process of Production," in *Capital – Volume I* (London: Penguin, 1990), 948–1084.
26   Marx, *Capital – Volume I* (New York: International Publishers, 1974), 509.

labour process is increasingly not the individual worker. Instead, *labour-power socially combined* and the various competing labour-powers, which together form the entire production machine participate in very different ways in the immediate process of making commodities, or, more accurately in this context, creating the product. Some work better with their hands, others with their heads, one as a manager, engineer, technologist, etc., the other as overseer, the third as manual labourer or even drudge. An ever-increasing number of types of labour are included in the immediate concept of *productive labour*, and those who perform it are classed as *productive workers*, workers directly exploited by capital and *subordinated* to its process of production and expansion. If we consider the aggregate *worker*, i.e. if we take all the members comprising the workshop together, then we see that their *combined activity* results materially in an *aggregate* product which is at the same time a *quantity of goods*. And here it is quite immaterial whether the job of a particular worker, who is merely a limb of this aggregate worker, is at a greater or smaller distance from the actual manual labour. But then: the activity of this aggregate labour-power is its *immediate productive consumption by capital*, i.e., it is the self-valorisation process of capital, and hence, as we shall demonstrate, the immediate production of surplus-value, the *immediate conversion of this latter into capital*.[27]

In this overview of the process of capital reproduction, which encompasses production as well as all moments of circulation (distribution, exchange and consumption), we conclude that the working class, *the source* of both production and capital valorisation (as well as of producing and reproducing its own labour power and with it, its very existence), replaces its salary (variable capital) and produces the surplus value that is appropriated *freely* by capital. In this logic, any worker who does not intervene in these functions as a member of the collective worker should therefore be considered an unproductive worker while the worker who indeed participates is understood to be a productive worker; one that belongs, therefore, to the working class, which at its core "... understands distinct types of workers and is organised in differentiated strata, in some of which its members are relocated 'to the margin' of the direct producers of value. However, involved as they are with the rest in the productive sphere, these are *member parts of the collective worker*."[28]

---

27   Marx, "Results," 1039–40.

28   Ruy Mauro Marini, "El concepto de trabajo productivo, nota metodológica," *Archivo de Ruy Mauro Marini*, 1993, accessed 16 April 2015, http://www.marini-escritos.unam .mx/078_trabajo_productivo.html.

Capitalism constantly strives to overcome all limitations that impede the mass build up of workers (collective worker) in the same space-time (factory). One such mechanism amongst so many others is the use of *cyberspace*, constructed by information and communication technologies that are able to overcome (virtually and relatively) the limitations of physical time and spatial-temporal differences between production centres and consumer markets. This has created a true revolution of total labour time, which in turn has lead to the expanded production of surplus value and an increase to the scale of capital accumulation as the exploitation of the collective worker deepens.

Conclusion

The labour process is the workshop in which value is produced and capital valorised. Of its three constituent elements (labour power, instruments of labour and the object of labour), only the first has the ability to create a new value that, specifically within the capitalist system, is converted to surplus labour or surplus value, which capital then appropriates. Without this imminent process of production, the system would enter inevitably into a pit of structural problems and crisis, which would make it unviable.

For this reason, it is important to distinguish variable capital from constant capital. Whereas the former varies in value as its generates new, additional value in the process of labour and exploitation, the latter—represented by fixed capital (machines, tools and buildings) and circulating capital (primary materials)—modifies neither its value nor its magnitude, but rather simply transfers its existing value to the final product, the commodity. But for this to occur, labour must be productive; in other words, it must possess the ability to produce surplus value. This is possible when the labour in question is articulated with the collective worker; a synthesis that defines socially-necessary labour for the production of value, or surplus value and of commodities in abstract terms, in a given society. Finally, only the proportion between the magnitudes of constant and variable capital (the organic composition of capital) changes through the expenditure of labour power. In this way, the validity of the labour theory of value is demonstrated in the manner by which it exposes how the *use value* of the worker's labour power creates value and surplus value, according to the established necessary labour time.

CHAPTER 3

The Structural Crisis of Capital and Abstract Labour

Introduction

This chapter argues that the crisis of capital is best understood as a crisis of abstract labour, which has ultimately been exposed in challenges related to the production of surplus value in the expanded conditions of reproduction required by capital accumulation. More than a mere financial, public sector deficit-related or housing crisis, we suggest that it is the *basis* of determining the value of commodities and labour power that has generated a series of structural obstacles to the production of value. This is encapsulated in the notion of the *dismeasure of value* which we use to suggest that the socially-necessary labour time of commodities is now insufficient to guarantee the mass of surplus value, and the shares of necessary surplus value, required by capital in order to maintain profitability under conditions of expansion.

Absolute and Relative Surplus Value

We saw that the *use value* of labour power (i.e., that which capital buys in the market) *produces surplus value*. We saw also that this value depends on socially-necessary labour time for its production and reproduction in a context where all individual labours are articulated in the collective worker, and where this labour time is the amount of wages that the worker will receive for her or his labour. As Marx writes, "The capitalist has bought the labour-power at its day-rate. To him its use-value belongs during one working-day."[1] For this same reason, he clarifies that, "The living labour time [the capitalist] gets in exchange is not the exchange value, but the use value of labour capacity."[2]

Thus, the frequent confusion between use value (which speaks to this capacity to create surplus value) and exchange value (which is expressed in the quantity of money that the worker receives in the form of a wage, which in turn is always less than the value of total capital) vanishes. Marx explains that in effect, "What the capitalist acquires through exchange is *labour capacity*:

---

1 Marx, *Capital – Volume I*, 1974, 232.

2 Marx, *Grundrisse*, 1993, 673.

this is the exchange value which he pays for."[3] The function of the use of labour power in production is also "the creation of abstract labour...and this use is carried out under capitalist direction."[4]

The category that ultimately defines capitalism is the wage; it is this that expresses the essential social relation at the level of the market, or the buying and selling of labour power conducted through capital. Thus "in the definition of the wage concept and its place in value theory, waged labour is character-ised as the product of a social relation, and therefore something generic and standard, which is the foundation of capitalism."[5] Before moving on to address the issue of labour super-exploitation, we must first review the concepts of absolute and relative surplus value. This issue first arises in the fourth section of the first volume of *Capital*, where one reads:

> The surplus-value produced by prolongation of the working-day, I call *absolute surplus-value*. On the other hand, the surplus-value arising from the curtailment of the necessary labour-time, and from the correspond-ing alteration in the respective lengths of the two components of the working-day, I call *relative surplus-value*. In order to effect a fall in the value of labour-power, the increase in the productiveness of labour must seize upon those branches of industry, whose products determine the value of labour-power, and consequently either belong to the class of cus-tomary means of subsistence, or are capable of supplying the place of those means.[6]

There are two methods of relative surplus value: first, when technological development directly affects the productive branches of sector II, which man-ufacture the means of life consumed by workers ('salary goods'); and secondly, when development operates indirectly in the productive branches of sector I, producing the means of production which in turn, through productive and labour chains, shape the productive branches of sector II (i.e., the means of consumption that determine the value of labour power, for example clothing, food, footwear and wood). In contrast to the concept of absolute surplus value (the extension of the working day), the particularity of relative surplus value lies in its relation to the means of production and technology, in so far as the latter tends to influence the branches of production that produce

---

3   Marx, *Grundrisse* (1993): 561–62.
4   Aglietta, *Regulación*, 29.
5   Aglietta, *Regulación*, 114.
6   Marx, *Capital – Volume I*, 315 (italics in original).

machinery and tools for sectors producing consumer goods which, in turn, provide the basic necessities normally consumed by the workforce. Thus, it becomes possible to reduce the value of labour power in keeping with the declining labour time required to produce a part or even all of these necessities. But if the increasing productive capacity of labour does *not* affect the productive branches of goods necessary for the maintenance of the worker then the value of labour power experiences no change whatsoever: "...an increase in the productiveness of labour in those branches of industry which supply neither the necessaries of life, nor the means of production for such necessaries, leaves the value of labour-power undisturbed."[7]

It is for this reason that capital will devote all effort and resources to producing relative surplus value by such means but, in the process, will inevitably be confronted by contradictions. By increasing relative surplus value and the time of unpaid surplus labour, capital reduces that part of labour leading to the social reproduction of the worker; in other words, the use value determined by socially-necessary labour time for its production, which is expressed in monetary proportion in the form of a wage.[8] And in the long term, the effect of these movements will be to reduce the *mass* of surplus value and therefore, the *rate* of surplus value, resulting in a fall in the rate of profit. This premise is illustrated in Table 3. Here, we see a gradual reduction of the portion corresponding to the value of labour spent (line a-b), and an increase to the portion corresponding to the worker's unpaid surplus labour that is appropriated by capital (line b-d), all without increasing the (absolute) magnitude of the working day. Essentially what is being expressed is a contradiction between its use value (concrete labour) and exchange value (abstract labour), since,

TABLE 3   *The working day (relative surplus value)*

a - - - - b - - - - c = 8 hours
a - - - b - - - - - c = 8 hours
a - - b - - - - - - c = 8 hours
a - b - - - - - - - c = 8 hours

Note: The line (a-b) corresponds to the value of labour power and its replacement, and is reflected in the wage. The line (b-c) represents the time of unpaid surplus labour, or surplus value

7   Marx, *Capital – Volume I*, 315 (italics in original).
8   Marx, *Capital – Volume I*, Chapter XII.

the very production of abstract labour implies a tendency to absorb increasingly less living labour per unit of dead labour. It is this that produces a tendency in the average rate of profit to fall to the detriment of gains in productivity, which constitutes the principle internal counter-tendency to this law. Thus, the very basis of the formation of value is undermined.[9]

However, to counteract this recessive tendency, the line (c) is extended until it reaches, for example, twelve, fourteen, fifteen or even seventeen hours daily or more (see Table 4).

But as the historical struggles of workers opposing this increment has shown, this method of producing *absolute surplus value* tends to provoke strong social conflicts both between workers and bosses, between fractions of capital, as well as inevitably with the very labour legislation protected (in theory, at least) by the State in the form of laws, regulations, contracts, clauses and rules. Nonetheless, capital will opt to extend the working day by means of diverse methods, such as overtime, shift work, and the violation of official working time. These measures have been widely used, and even more so in times of crisis, as we now see in many countries of the world, including those of the European Union.[10] Crucially, this practice combines with relative surplus value, since it is only with this "that the subsumption of production under the categories of capitalism arise, an issue that constitutes a specific characteristic of our age."[11]

TABLE 4   *The working day (absolute surplus value)*

a - - - - b - - - - c = 8 hours
a - - - - b - - - - c - - - - d = 12 hours (a + b + c)
a - - - - b - - - - c - - - - - - d= 14 hours (a + b + c)
a - - - - b - - - - c - - - - - - - - d = 16 hours

Note: The line (c-d) represents the extension of the working day beyond the legal limit

---

9   Alain Bihr, "Las formas concretas del trabajo abstracto," *Revista Herramienta* (Buenos Aires) 44 (2010): 37.
10   This last alternative, approved by ministers of the European Union, was a move to increase the working week up to 65 hours. All that remains is for the provision to be ratified by national parliaments which incidentally, have little weight against the supreme ministerial decisions of the union.
11   Alves, *A condição de proletariedade*, 196.

Aglietta offers a clear caution to those who hold that an antagonistic relation exists between absolute and relative surplus value when he writes that "absolute and relative value are inseparable. They create the necessity for capitalism to continually transform the conditions of production."[12] Marini makes a similar point, arguing that in dependent capitalism

> ...technical progress enabled the capitalist to intensify the rhythm of labour, to elevate the worker's productivity while, at the same time, maintaining the tendency to pay him or her at a lower rate than his or her real value.[13]

A third mechanism used by capital in the production of surplus value is to increase the *intensity of labour* such that the magnitudes of the working day are left unchanged but the production of value and surplus value are intensified.[14] It is worth noting here that, by 'labour intensity,' we mean increases to production entailing the physical and psychological exhaustion of the worker within a discrete space and time (e.g., one hour, eight hours, or one year) without entailing substantial technological development of the means of production, instruments or socio-technical organisation of work.

This method is closely bounded with modern organisational processes both in the labour process as well as commodity production (e.g., automobile, shipyards, furniture, canning, car seats, clothing) based on the Toyota system of flexible production. Dal Rosso associates the intensity of labour with relative surplus value[15] in the following terms:

> Formalizing this intensification in keeping with the concept of surplus value, the Toyotist system would be a combined example of type iii of relative surplus value; that is, one in which technological changes

---

12   Aglietta, *Regulación*, 35.

13   Ruy Mauro Marini, *Dialéctica de la dependencia* (Ciudad de México: Ediciones Era, 1973), 72. This is the essence of Marini's approach to labour super-exploitation, which we examine at a later point.

14   We should clarify that only when the increasing intensity of labour is generalised to all branches of production, and effectively influences the devaluation of labour power, can we say that it produces additional surplus value. When this has not occurred, the *individual capital operating in the productive branch where rising intensity has taken place has only managed to produce extraordinary surplus value following a decline in the unit value of its products.*

15   Sadi Dal Rosso, *Mais trabalho. A intensificação do labor na sociedade contemporânea* (São Paulo: Boitempo Editorial, 2008), 47 *et seq.*

combine with transformations in the organisation of work to contribute to an increase [in the mass of surplus value].[16]

In addition, the author identifies two additional forms of intensity: the first is associated with technological change in the productive process[17] and the second is derived from the organisation of work rather than from the industrial revolution per se, as in the former.[18]

In the process of attempting to produce surplus value and increase the rate of profit, capital strives to articulate these three forms of labour intensity, linked to relative as well as absolute surplus value. *In practice, these mechanisms converge in the self-valorisation of capital* in so far as they are always amenable to any circumstance, market fluctuation and inter-capitalist competition faced by businesses. As Mészáros maintains,

> Neither the degradation of nature nor the pain of social devastation carries any meaning at all for its system of social metabolic control when set against the absolute imperative of self-reproduction on an ever-extended scale.[19]

In this way, the ideal of capital, which consists in the drive to reduce dead time as much as possible, the *porosity* of the working day and waste in production (with *just in time* systems and the like), in order to counteract the crisis of overproduction (which represents moments of devalorisation of, and so losses for, capital) finds a relative, momentary solution in the Toyotist system and these methods of combined exploitation.

As a tool in the production of relative surplus value, the scientific-technological revolution (in information technologies, telematics, microelectronics, communications, biogenetics) squeezes socially-necessary labour time *when and only when* it fundamentally affects the consumption by workers, in relation to living labour (in the earlier schema, the line represented by a-b) and by increasing the time of unpaid surplus labour that represents surplus value (line b-c). It is a law of capital to reduce the line a-b in order to increase that of c-d:

> The object of all development of the productiveness of labour, within the limits of capitalist production, is to shorten that part of the working-day,

---

16   Dal Rosso, *Mais trabalho*, 70.

17   Ibid., 47.

18   Ibid., 63.

19   Mészáros, *Beyond Capital: Towards a Theory of Transition* (New York: Monthly Review, 1995), 173.

during which the workman must labour for his own benefit, and by that very shortening, to lengthen the other part of the day, during which he is at liberty to work gratis for the capitalist.[20]

The above reinforces the fact that socially-necessary labour time depends on the development of the productive forces and the degree of skill, productivity and average intensity of the workforce.[21] The exploitation of the workforce through the production of relative surplus value is therefore essentially hegemonic, if not exclusively so:

> Moreover, in recent decades, strategies of extracting relative surplus value in the production of capital have spread with greater intensity and depth as a way to restore profit margins by increasing the average rate of exploitation; flexible accumulation and Toyotism are organisational forms of capital innovation that contain this disruptive spirit, reconstituting, as such, the 'capture of labour subjectivity.'[22]

Relative surplus value, based on the industrial revolution and the incorporation of technology into the labour process, has faced increasing difficulties in the effort to expand.[23] While the author cited does not recognise a crisis in relative surplus value as such, and rather speaks of its spread as a means of restoring the margins of rates of profit by increasing the average rate of exploitation, we believe that within the framework of relative surplus labour and its crisis, it is rather the super-exploitation of labour that has taken the lead in recovering these margins. And this is precisely because the productive system can no longer create a sufficient mass of surplus value (the basis of the production and appropriation of profits) to reproduce itself on an ever-increasing scale within the market system. And here we arrive at the core of the cause of the current crisis: as much as living labour (expended labour power) has been reduced by dismissals, the substitution of human labour by machines (what Antunes, following Juan J. Castillo, has called 'organisational lyophilisation')[24] or by whatever other method, the global aggregate value produced in a given society and the absolute mass of surplus value (which ultimately determine

20   Marx, *Capital – Volume I*, 321.

21   Marini, "Laz razones," 64.

22   Alves, *A condição*, 180–81.

23   Alves, *A condição*, 180 *et seq.*

24   Ricardo Antunes, *The Meanings of Work: Essay on the Affirmation and Negation of Work*, trans. Elizabeth Molinari (Leiden: Brill, 2013), 34.

the amount of profit) have been reduced. From this stems a contradiction: on the one hand, capital searches all avenues to substitute the living force of labour for machinery, regardless of the form it takes, while on the other hand it cannot completely do without living labour, other than by risking its own valorisation and ultimately the production of surplus value. In effect, as Amorim puts it, "historically, capital tended to limit and reduce its dependency on labour, but it could never do so completely for it depends on its exploitation to generate surplus value."[25] The authors of the *Manifesto against Labour* have also denounced this trend:

> With the third industrial revolution of microelectronics, the labour society reached its absolute historical barrier. That this barrier would be reached sooner or later was logically foreseeable. From birth, the commodity-producing system suffers from a fatal contradiction in terms. On the one hand, it lives on the massive intake of human energy generated by the expenditure of pure labour power—the more the better. On the other hand, the law of operational competition enforces a permanent increase in productivity bringing about the replacement of human labour power by scientific operational industrial capital.[26]

The authors conclude that the root cause of capitalist crisis, such as that which shook the United States during the great crash of 1929–1933, lies in this contradiction.

On the other hand, the phenomenon caused by the crisis of relative surplus value has been translated into a strengthening of fictitious capital[27] which is driving a decline in the average growth rate of the global productive system. Over the medium and long term, this has led to a fall in the average rate of profit, a trend which plunged capitalism into the most severe economic crisis in the first decade of the 21st century. This has also resulted in an enormous

25   Henrique Amorim, *Trabalho imaterial: Marx e o debate contemporánio* (São Paulo: FAPESP, Annablume Editora, 2009), 17–18.

26   Robert Kurz, Norbert Trenkle and Ernst Lohoff, "Manifesto against Labour," *Krisis: Kritik der Warengesellschaft*, 31 December 1999, accessed 28 September 2014, http://www.krisis .org/1999/manifesto-against-labour.

27   *Fictitious capital*, as the movement involving all other forms that the cycle of international capital takes (such as money capital, productive capital and merchant capital), is defined as "so much currency" [TN: "simples medios de circulación imaginários" in the Spanish edition. Marx, Karl, *El capital, Libro III* (Ciudad de México: Fondo de Cultura Económica, 2000), 382] which J.W. Bosanquet (*Metallic, Paper and Credit Currency*, London, 1842) in his time identified as occurring "in detriment of productive capital." Marx, *Capital – Volume III*, 401.

concentration and centralisation of monetary and financial capital in the United States as well as in virtually all other countries who are paying down a growing debt.[28]

If the line a-b is constantly reduced until it reaches zero (an absurd proposition, but statistically possible), capitalism would collapse like a house of cards and cease to produce value since the only force capable of creating it is the human, living labour power of the collective worker. As Mészáros suggests, "Fantasies about the coming of totally automated and worker-free capitalist production process are generated as an imaginary elimination of this problem."[29] In fact, the problem continues without resolution. *Eppur si muove.*

The Crisis of Relative Surplus Value, the Dismeasure of Value, and the Devalorisation of Labour Power

Many authors have broached the structural crisis of capital by addressing the relation between concrete and abstract labour, as categories that encapsulate numerous issues relating to the modes of production of surplus value in contemporary capitalism.[30] The discussion identifies certain difficulties that Marx anticipated regarding the production of surplus value and its implications for capitalist reproduction and crisis. Alves discusses the structural crisis of capitalism beginning from the crisis of abstract labour which, he argues, is a sign of precisely the *effect* of relative surplus value on the system, in the following terms:

> ...the crisis of abstract labour and its reflexive derivations (the structural precarisation of labour and the financialisation of capitalist wealth) is paradoxically a candid expression of the degree to which relative surplus value is fully in force. The capitalism of full-scale industry is that of relative surplus value, which entails in and of itself a tendency towards increasing the organic composition of capital and a declining average

---

28   On 31 January 2011, in the United States, "the total public debt reached more than US$14 trillion with signs that it would reach $15 trillion by the end of 2011." Jorge Moreira, "La batalla contra el gobierno antidemocrático del estado de Wisconsin," *Rebelión*, 28 February 2011, accessed 28 September 2014, http://www.rebelion.org/noticia.php?id=123317.

29   Mészáros, *Beyond Capital* (New York: Monthly Review, 1995), 66.

30   The Argentinean journal *Herramienta* dedicated its volume 44 (June 2010) to this debate, with contributions by Alain Bihr, Werner Bonefeld and Roberto Follari, amongst others.

rate of profit on a global scale (with the historical counter-tendencies mentioned above).[31]

Here a paradox (if not a contradiction) seems to appear that we can formulate as follows: Is the crisis of abstract labour the result of relative surplus value being in full force, as the author maintains? Or rather, are the growing difficulties and contradictions experienced in the production of relative surplus value, as we suggest, factors that explain the crisis of abstract labour? This brings us to the central thesis of the present book: *the crisis of relative surplus value is the essence of the structural crisis of capital in advanced capitalism. As such, it has become possible for labour super-exploitation to become generalised throughout the system (with specific modalities, to be sure) as the counterpart both of the crisis of relative surplus value and of the tendentious fall in the average rate of profit, and the implications this holds for other categories such as rent, inflation, taxation and unemployment.*

We must distinguish two concepts directly related to the logic of capitalist reproduction. The first is the 'dismeasure of value' used by scholars of the *Grundrisse*, and the second, the devalorisation of labour power which relates to the concept of relative surplus value. With respect to the first, in his book *The Immaterial*, André Gorz highlights contradictions internal to the dynamic of capital that surface in the fact that the social wealth produced by the workforce increasingly conflicts with the logic of commodity exchange value and, as a result, can no longer be measured by conventional quantitative and rational criteria. In relation to the speculative bubble, as the author thus writes that,

> ...it is difficult for the capitalist system to transform (monetary) value and to make the value of 'immaterial capitalism' (which is by definition immeasurable and non-exchangeable) function as capital, in order to position 'cognitive capitalism' as capitalism in general. The monetary equivalences of both assets and intangible goods no longer measure anything that is measureable. They reflect a relation of forces, not relations of equivalence.[32]

---

31   Giovanni Alves, "Crise de valorização e desmedida do capital. Breve ensaio sobre a natureza da crise estrutural do capital," in *Capital trabajo y nueva organización obrera*, edited by Esthela Gutiérrez, Didimo Castillo and Adrián Sotelo (Ciudad de México: Siglo XXI Editores, 2011), 31.

32   André Gorz, *O Imaterial: conhecimento, valor e capital* (São Paulo: Annablume Editora, 2005), 23.

At one level, Marx understood this as a contradiction between the socialisation of material productive forces and the dominant forms and mechanisms of their private appropriation under the rule of exchange value ($c + v + sv$). For Gorz, however, the hegemony that so-called immaterial labour (which generates the 'dismeasure of value,' under which labour time no longer functions as the mechanism of the measure of value, and labour, the measure of social wealth) has acquired in society leads him to throw out Marx's labour theory of value entirely in favour of other categories such as immaterial labour, information, science, and technology.[33]

The second concept (the 'devalorisation of labour power') reflects a more sophisticated internal contradiction which, rather than stemming from relative surplus value, begins when the movement of capital and its valorisation begin to conflict with value-producing labour power. While in the first instance (the 'dismeasure of value') the value produced loses its point of reference and measure under the logic of capital, in the second instance value production has eroded the very material basis that sustains the production of value through the devaluing of labour power, which also has material and historical-moral limits beyond which the production of value and surplus value would cease. This was demonstrated by Marx in Chapter IX of volume I of Capital where he assumes that constant capital (c, referring to the means of production) is equal to zero, while variable capital (v) is limited to reproducing the equivalent of its own value: ($c = [o + v] = v$), and where C^1 (capital valorised) = $v + sv$, and $C^1 = sv$, remains exactly as before. Conversely if sv is o (in other words, if the labour power whose value is spent in variable capital only produces its equivalent), we would have $C = c + v$, and C^1 (the value of the product) = $(c + v) + o$. Therefore, $C = C^1$ and the invested capital would not have produced any additional value.[34]

As we saw earlier, responsibility for the production of new value (the equivalent of expended labour power plus surplus value), as well as the conservation and transference of the value of the means of production, falls entirely to labour power in light of its *double character* as the producer of value. The most suitable method found to date is the production of *relative surplus value* under the exploitation of labour and increased productivity which, over the long term, conflicts with the immanent requirements of valorisation and increasing the rate of profit, both of which are vital to securing the expanded reproduction of the system as a whole.

---

33   See André Gorz, *Miseria del presente, riqueza de lo posible* (Buenos Aires: Paidós, 1998).

34   Marx, *Capital – Volume I*, 213–14.

Recent advances in science and technology have enhanced these two contradictions. As we argue here, these in turn have put the production of value
and surplus value in check. As such, while the system remains grounded in the
capitalist mode of production and its basic categories (exploitation, private
property, capitalist appropriation, valorisation, monopoly, as well as the logic
of the *social metabolism of capital*), it has proven necessary to *extend labour
super-exploitation* to the point that it becomes a universal process; one imposed
to sustain the production of value and the regime of commodity production,
the production of surplus value and increasing profits. The growing challenge
of producing surplus value on a scale sufficient to guarantee the expanded
reproduction of capital has spurred a further series of contradictions, as
reflected in the concept of *problematic valorisation*,

> ...on the scale of the global market...which explains the capitalist offen-
> sive against the rights of workers in industrialized countries, seeking to
> increase the global rate of exploitation of the workforce.[35]

Problematic valorisation acts to stimulate the technological revolution, intensifying the structural contradictions of capitalism which, over the long-term,
will only be resolved through social struggle and political processes such as
those currently unfolding all over the world.

The notion of the 'dismeasure of value' emerges from the tendency of capital to turn labour into immaterial labour and so, from a position that sees
immaterial labour as its cause.[36] But here is it important to signal that, in contrast to authors such as Gorz, Lazzarato and Negri, from our point of view,
immaterial labour is inextricably linked to the cycle of material labour. In so far
as the former can be explained by the latter, the labour theory of value and its
corresponding ontological and conceptual categories remain valid. Other
approaches have suggested that, in light of the supposed hegemony that immaterial labour has acquired in society, it is necessary to elaborate a new law of
value. This is clear in Hardt and Negri when they write,

> The central role previously occupied by the labor power of mass factory
> workers in the production of surplus value is today increasingly filled by
> intellectual, immaterial, and communicative labor power. It is thus nec-
> essary to develop a new political theory of value that can pose the prob-
> lem of this new capitalist accumulation of value at the center of the

---

35   Alves, "Crise estrutural," 55.
36   Alves, *A condição*, 33.

mechanism of exploitation (and thus, perhaps, at the center of potential revolt).[37]

Hardt and Negro suppose that immaterial labour (a pillar of *empire*) is currently hegemonic both in society and in the process of commodity production; on this basis, they back the 'need' for a new theory of value and subjectivity based on 'knowledge, communication and language.'[38] Staying closely to the Habermasian theory of communication, the authors maintain that

> [t]his industrial context provides a first sense in which communication and information have come to play a newly central role in production. One might say that instrumental action and communicative action have become intimately interwoven in the informationalized industrial process, but one should quickly add that this is an impoverished notion of communication as the mere transmission of market data.[39]

Clearly, there lacks a more profound discussion of the effects of communication and information technology, both in relation to the material process of commodity production and, more importantly, to the production of surplus value, which might broaden the conception of industrial production or modern big industry.

Similarly Lazzarato and Negri suggest that, "Immaterial labour tends to become hegemonic, in a totally explicit way," but do not clarify the processes and characteristics by which this is achieved.[40] They argue that we have reached a stage of immaterial labour embodied, according to the authors, in personality, subjectivity, and the very soul of contemporary society. It is perhaps this which leads the authors to conceptualise a *social cycle* specific to production in the 'diffused factory'—the decentralised organisation of labour and varied outsourced forms of production—a concept from which derives the following thesis:

---

37 Michael Hardt & Antonio Negri, *Empire* (London: Harvard University Press, 2002), 29. For a critique of their central thesis, see Amorim, *Trabalho inmaterial*, particularly Chapter 2, pp. 75–117.

38 Hardt & Negri, *Empire*, 29.

39 Hardt & Negri, *Empire*, 290.

40 Maurizio Lazzarato and Antonio Negri, *Trabajo inmaterial. Formas de vida y producción de subjetividad, Rebelión*, 2 December 2002, accessed 11 October 2014, http://www.rebelion.org/noticia.php?id=121986 [Originally published in Rio de Janeiro: DP&A Editora, 2001.].

> ...the *cycle* of immaterial labour is predicated on a *social and autonomous* labour power, capable of organizing its own work and social relations with the firm. No scientific organisation of labour can predetermine this capacity and productive social capacity.[41]

This exaggerated understanding of the frequency of immaterial labour in contemporary society and in productive processes, beyond its mistaken conception as a standalone process with no connection with material labour, ignores the existence of millions of workers in the dependent countries of the Third World. Such workers, to the degree that they are affected by the introduction of new information and communication technologies (developed in the centres of research and development in industrialised countries), remain subject to the materiality of exploitation, structural relations, and cyclical determinants of capital in relation to wages, living and working conditions, and ultimately in such countries, the social value of a workforce that is generally paid below its value.

From our point of view, it is not correct to speak of a 'distinct cycle' of immaterial production and labour as though it were a hermetically sealed compartment of capitalist production, because what we are really talking about is a globally interconnected system that involves diverse kinds of labour (material and immaterial, cognitive, manual, simple and complex) which are incorporated and subsumed under the aegis of relative surplus value and the logic of the rate of profit. The capitalist mode of production, as a global system interconnected through social relations of production and material productive force, quashes any notion of the existence of an exclusively 'immaterial cycle' of labour operating outside or above the labour theory of value. Hence,

> ...the concept of a 'process (or cycle) of immaterial production' is misleading. In truth, there is a *capitalist process of labour, a living complex of labour that combines material labour and immaterial labour within.* It is a conceptual fantasy to allow a pure kind of immaterial labour, as it is a disjunction between material and immaterial labour.[42]

We hold that immaterial labour, as a product of the social collective, is a contradictory expression of abstract labour (which determines the formation of value and surplus value beginning with the exploitation of labour power) that at the same time reaffirms the existence of material labour which, in turn,

---

41   Lazzarato & Negri, *Trabalho inmaterial,* 11.
42   Alves, "Crise estrutural," 70.

displays the interlinked cognitive and manual aspects of the collective human capacity to work. Here, for example,

> This uniform character of labour, consisting of being a part of *global* labour in a society, is called *abstract labour*... Abstract labour is a social relation that transforms the products of labour into classes of equivalences (of a homogenous space within which a measure called value can be defined) called commodities. Thus it is correct to say that commodities have a value, just as it is correct to say that the material bodies that are subject to the gravity have a weight.[43]

In capitalist society there is no purely manual, material or physical labour that is disconnected from intellectual or immaterial work. In reality, both dimensions of social labour are encapsulated in corporality, intelligence and the very humanity of the workforce, even when observed in the most basic activity (for example, grinding stones, picking up litter, cleaning factory machinery or laying bricks in the construction of buildings). On the other hand, immaterial labour, just like material work, is also subject to the essential contradictions of capitalism and to trends pointing to the displacement of 'labour time' (the axis around which values and prices of production of commodities were previously calculated) under the impact of what was previously called the *dismeasure of value.*

This has provoked a situation in which labour time enters into a state of tension, and subsequently crisis, generating new problems for the reproduction of capital starting from the creation of surplus value and profits that depend on the *limit* of labour time. As Marx writes, 'Moments are the elements of profit.'[44] In this context, the constant challenge facing the *symbolic analyst of capitalism* (which immaterial labour represents, for certain authors) is how to increase the rate of exploitation (the relation between socially-necessary labour time and unpaid surplus labour time, key to the formation of surplus value). It is worth noting that socially-necessary labour time is determined by the degree of productive development and by the average degree of stress, productivity and intensity of labour power which are interrelated processes.[45]

Marx's scientific projection for the 19th century (which we consider to be valid for the 21st century and the *essential* explication of the contemporary crisis) suggests that the clash between labour time and the *dismeasure of value*

---

43   Aglietta, *Regulación*, 22.

44   Marx, *Capital – Volume I*, 243.

45   Marini, "Las razones," 64.

in capitalism will only deepen as it takes hold throughout the system. One angle of this problem can be seen in the increase to labour productivity, which usually leads to relative surplus value following the application of advanced technologies to the productive processes and the organisation of labour, amongst other things; this occurs by significantly reducing the value of labour power through the reduction of the unit-prices and the value of the workers' consumption fund. Thus, 'socially-necessary labour time' is no longer sufficient ground in capital's effort to increase surplus value, and over the long term, the rate of profit, which to the contrary tends to decline. The declining rate of profit in turn stimulates the extension of speculative processes of fictitious capital throughout the system, and the concentration and centralisation of capital to the benefit of dominant companies both in advanced and in dependent, underdeveloped capitalism. As a result, financial, monetary, housing, and food crises have been unleashed with alarming frequency, all ultimately following serious and profound imbalances of production and capital valorisation. While the average social and necessary labour time has certainly grown in this period, it has done so in a linear and increasingly lower rate, due to the displacement of the workforce by machinery, technology, primary materials (amongst other things) which, as we suggested in Chapter 2, create neither value nor surplus value but, rather, only transfer them to the commodity.

In effect, if capital broadens its range of activities to invest in new machinery, structures, stores or branches, and workforces, and if it is centralised in very few monopolies (transnational companies), this is due to the inexorable expropriation of many capitals by more powerful ones. It subsequently becomes possible to reduce the technical composition of capital at the cost of reducing the need to invest in variable capital which generates a decline in the demand for labour and increasing unemployment. The result of this entire shift is that the amount of surplus value will decline (and even when it appears to grow, it will do so at a marginal rate), meaning that an historical-structural limit has been reached which capital will have to overcome in order to ensure its continuing expansion. Marx discusses this in the *Grundrisse*:

> The larger the surplus value of capital *before the increase of productive force*, the larger the amount of presupposed surplus labour or surplus value of capital; or, the smaller the fractional part of the working day which forms the equivalent of the worker, which expresses necessary labour, the smaller is the increase in surplus value which capital obtains from the increase of productive forces. Its surplus value rises, but in an ever smaller relation to the development of the productive force. Thus the more developed capital already is, the more surplus labour it has

created, the more terribly must it develop the productive force in order to realize itself in only smaller proportion, i.e., to add surplus value— because its barrier always remains the relation between the fractional part of the day which expresses *necessary labour*, and the entire working day. It can move only within these boundaries. The smaller already the fractional part falling to *necessary labour*, the greater the *surplus labour*, the less can any increase in productive force perceptibly diminish necessary labour; since the denominator has grown enormously. The self-realization of capital becomes more difficult to the extent that it has already been realized. The increase of productive force would become irrelevant to capital; realization itself would become irrelevant, because its proportions have become minimal, and it would have ceased to be capital. ... But this happens not because wages have increased or the share of labour in the product, but because it has *already* fallen so low, regarded in its relation to the product of labour or to the living working day.[46]

In this paragraph, Marx emphasises two moments in the production of surplus value and socially-necessary labour time that relate dialectically to the dynamic of productive forces (pf) in society:

From Table 5, we can infer the following: first, the graphic illustrates that in both cases (as we signalled earlier) there is always the possibility that capital will rely on an absolute increase to the working day (prolonging the line b-c but within certain limits). Indeed, this occurs in the context of everyday practices associated with labour exploitation; however, in the second instance, this

TABLE 5   *8-hour working day (hypothetical)*

Production of surplus value before an increase to the productive forces (pf)	Production of surplus value following an increase to the productive forces (pf)
a - - - - b - - - - c	a - - - - b - - - - c
a - - - b - - - - - c	a - - b - - - - - - c
a - - b - - - - - - c	a - b - - - - - - - c
a - b - - - - - - - c	If $a + b = 0$, then $b - c = 0$ (the production of sv collapses)

---

46   Marx, *Grundrisse*, 340–41.

increase occurs in combination with relative surplus value. It is assumed that, where there has been no improvement made to the productive forces, any increase of st and decrease of nt are a result of procedures related to absolute surplus value, to the intensity of labour and/or to the super-exploitation of the workforce (which combines the previous two processes with compensating labour power below its value, which we analyse later in Chapter 5). To the contrary, with an increase of the productive force, the hegemonic regime being imposed is in fact relative surplus value, particularly when it contributes to diminishing the quantity of socially-necessary labour in the reproduction of labour power and, therefore, necessary labour time. We anticipate that the super-exploitation of labour, in such a regime, does not vanish in dependent economies simply by virtue of the fact that relative surplus value has become prominent. Rather, the latter imposes its logic (but not its hegemony) on the production and accumulation of capital, albeit in a narrow manner, particularly in those periods of intensive industrialisation of the sort that took place in the largest economies of Latin American countries in the final quarter of the 20th century including Mexico, Brazil and Argentina, all of which significantly improved their industrial indicators following the Second World War.[47]

Secondly, in the first case (without an increase in productivity), nt decreases and st increases so that additions to the working day are more frequent, while in the second case (*with* an increase in productivity) the opposite occurs, in so far as the increase of productive capacity affects a devalorisation of products and services which make up the value of labour power, thus increasing the mass of surplus value.

Third, the *qualitative difference*, from a theoretical and categorical point of view, stems from the impact of the development of the productive forces on both magnitudes: while in the first case every increase of productive force results in the greater exploitation of the worker and, subsequently, an increase of surplus labour, in the second case we see that greater productivity reduces socially-necessary labour time; and also that, while increasing surplus labour and surplus value over the long term, each increase of the productive forces (through scientific and technological development) spurs a *decline* in the growth of surplus value. In other words, such growth becomes increasingly marginal until it reaches a structural limit in which it must cease production due to the extreme reduction of socially-necessary labour time (i.e., corresponding to the value of labour power and its reproduction,

---

47   See Adrián Sotelo Valencia, *Desindustrialización y crisis del neoliberalismo. Maquiladoras y telecomunicaciones* (Ciudad de México: Plaza y Valdés, 2004).

and also, to that which is the only commodity with the capacity to create surplus value).

These considerations, addressed in the *Grundrisse*, are taken up and developed in *Capital*, but now in the form of a law:

> In general, the greater the productiveness of labour, the less is the labour-time required for the production of an article, the less is the amount of labour crystallised in that article, and the less is its value; and *vice versa*, the less the productiveness of labour, the greater is the labour-time required for the production of an article, and the greater is its value. The value of a commodity, therefore, varies directly as the quantity, and inversely as the productiveness, of the labour incorporated in it.[48]

Hence, the significance of Marx's thesis regarding the development of productive forces through technical progress constitutes the core of his theory and operates with the force of law in the capitalist system: "The increase of productive force would become irrelevant to capital."[49] What does this mean? The proposition we have before us is that, as much as capital revolutionises its means of production and transport, applying science and technology to productive processes and the labour process, capital is unable to significantly increase the production of value and surplus value (even while able to destroy nature and the productive forces of society) by these means alone; a point that brings the system to the brink of disaster with stagnation, deep recessions and predatory barbarity.

Elaborating on the effects of the reduction of socially-necessary labour time on the production of surplus value, Mészáros bluntly contends that,

> The point is that in order to extricate itself from the difficulties of profitable expansion and accumulation globally competing capital tends to reduce to a profitable minimum 'necessary labour time' (or the 'labour cost of production'), thereby inevitably tending to transform the workers into an increasingly *superfluous labour force*. But by doing so capital

---

48   Marx, *Capital – Volume 1*, 40. Later, we will see how the addition of productive capacity does not reduce, but rather intensifies, labour super-exploitation once dependent capitalism enters the sphere of relative surplus value and enhanced labour productivity; particularly, over the course of industrialisation in the 1950s.

49   Marx, *Grundrisse*, 340–41.

simultaneously undermines the vital conditions of its own expanded reproduction.[50]

The author emphasises that this contradiction between reduced nt and st (ingrained in the social metabolism of capital) is inherent to the law of value, and that it has remained throughout "the 'maturation' or full assertion of the law of value under conditions marked by the closure of the progressive phase of capital's historical ascendancy."[51] On the other hand, it also reveals the current difficulty of the law of value to operate within the structural limits of the general system of capital. Crucially, it reaffirms an essential contradiction of the capitalist system, which speaks to what others have called capital's 'destructive uncontrollability' in the absence of a socialist alternative.[52]

In light of the above, the hypothesis we are putting forward is the following: *the more that productivity continues to increase, driving the technological, 'labour saving' revolution* (with the resulting unemployment, lowering of real wages, growth of the industrial reserve army and destruction of productive jobs), *the more difficult, fragile and marginal will socially-necessary labour time become in the production of commodities and reproduction of the workforce. It will become increasingly insignificant for the production of sufficient value and surplus value, even though it increases the general volume of physical wealth (use values) in society, it does so with progressively less value contained therein.* As such, as we now see taking place, the system will enter into an organic, structural and civilisational crisis.

The Capitalist Crisis as a Crisis of Value and Surplus Value

In this conceptual framework, the current crisis in capitalist society is not a housing crisis; it is not a financial or monetary crisis; it is not a crisis of energy or food security; it is not a crisis of trade and overproduction. The crisis is the product of all of the above rather than simply one thing or another, as neoliberal experts and international organisms generally suggest when they reduce such factors to the spheres of circulation, particularly to monetary and financial problems. This is, at its essence, a crisis of the capitalist mode of production grounded in the hegemony of fictitious capital, an enormously dynamic speculative capital that

---

50   Mészáros, *Beyond Capital*, 150–51 (italics in the original). For this author neither "globalisation" nor the expansion of monopolies and greater intensity to the labour process guarantees an exit to this 'vicious cycle' per se.

51   Mészáros, *Beyond Capital*, 151.

52   Ibid.

greatly informs social wealth, but whose reinvestment in the productive sphere is, in and of itself, insufficient for the expanded reproduction of capital.

As such, it is a crisis of surreptitious mechanisms of value and surplus value production that centralise capital in the financial-speculative sphere, in the hands of banks and stock exchanges, with the objective of driving increases in the rate of profit. The result of this dynamic is to enrich an increasingly smaller proportion of the world's population, as indicated by the fact that 39% of global wealth is now concentrated in the hands of less than 1% of the global population;[53] in the United States, 10% of the most wealthy have captured 81% of the country's income.[54]

It is *structural* because it operates within structures of accumulation and capital reproduction required for its self-valorisation, and it is *systemic* in so far as it pervades capital's operations and gives shape to its social metabolism in a global, comprehensive sense. It is *contradictory* because in each cycle of crisis and expansion, new contradictions and imbalances are generated which are becoming increasingly irresolvable over time: strong tendencies which drive down the rate of profit; movements against greater production of value and surplus value; the incessant growth of unemployment, underemployment and poverty; concentration and centralisation of capital, inflation and the unleashing of imperialist wars against underdeveloped nations (see Table 6). While appearing superficially as a 'financial crisis,' especially a crisis of the hegemony of fractions of the global financial oligarchy using the banks and stock exchanges under their control, the current capitalist crisis,

TABLE 6   *Global crisis of capital*

1. *Structural*: Permanent and progressive.
2. *Systemic*: Operating within each cycle of production: the tendency towards the reduction of growth processes, the development of capital, and spatial-temporal prolongation of processes associated with recession and crisis.
3. *Contradictory*: Tendencies of rupture within cycles of capital and eruptions of prolonged and intense crises.

53 Boston Consulting Group, "Market Sizing: Capitalizing on a Sustained Recovery," from Global Wealth 2011: Shaping a New Tomorrow, accessed 29 August 2015, https://www .bcgperspectives.com/content/articles/financial_institutions_pricing_global_wealth _2011_shaping_new_tomorrow/?chapter=2#chapter2_section3.

54 Michel Husson, "A Crisis without End," *International Viewpoint*, 8 August 2011, accessed 6 April 2015, http://www.internationalviewpoint.org/spip.php?article2236.

...exploded with the financial debacle. [But behind] it unfolded a crisis of the real economy, or rather a relative stagnation of production, and what this will lead to is the regression of earnings of workers, increasing work stoppages, greater precariousness and worsening poverty in the countries of the South.[55]

The above traits reveal the crisis of the economic system as one involving the production of value and surplus value.

Marx developed this thesis in the *Grundrisse*, which would later appear in *Capital*.[56] In both settings, the thesis laid the groundwork for a materialist theory of capitalist development and its decadence to illustrate that only human labour, the labour power of the worker, creates value and surplus value and is able to enhance the value of the capital invested.[57] Rather than machinery, technology, tools, money or land, only human labour, the *living force* of labour in the process of valorisation, can create value: "...capital creates no surplus value as long as it employs no living labour. The reproduction of the employed fixed capital itself is of course not the positing of surplus value,"[58] in so far as its role is limited to transferring a portion of its own value.

The impossibility of capital generating surplus value *without* labour power, as certain illustrious intellectuals believe, explains the fall in the rate of profit, which becomes clear as technology and machinery are incorporated into the production process.[59] Harman puts it as follows:

Marx argued that over time competition forces capitalists to invest in more and more dead labour—so each worker sets in motion a greater mass of machinery and raw materials. But if the total amount of dead labour rises, while the living labour (the source of profit) stays the same,

---

55 Alonso Aguilar, "En torno a la crisis actual," in *La crisis actual del capitalismo* (Ciudad de México: Comité Coordinador del Centro Mexicano de Estudios Sociales, Siglo XXI Editores, 2011), 15.

56 Roman Rosdolsky, *Génesis y estructura de* El capital *de Marx. Estudios sobre los Grundrisse* (Ciudad de México: Siglo XXI Editores, 1978).

57 In *The Poverty of Philosophy* of 1847, the materialist conception of the labour theory of value on which Marx would base his latter works takes form. See Karl Marx, *The Poverty of Philosophy* (Moscow: Progress Publishers, 1975).

58 Marx, *Grundrisse*, 670.

59 We should stress that if technology *affects* the consumption fund of the worker, which reproduces the value of his or her labour power, in this case the productive forces improve and the production of relative surplus value takes place.

the capitalist will invest more but get the same profit. Hence the rate of profit will fall.[60]

The crisis manifests as a failure of the potential mechanisms of the system to generate sufficient value in the labour process, to valorise the capital invested (i.e., the means of production, primary materials and in the workforce, or variable capital), and to create surplus value and restore the rate of profit. These limitations provoke a deviation to the speculative spheres of financial-fictitious capital, and contribute to the formation of speculative bubbles in areas such as housing, energy and foodstuffs.[61] In this last instance (which directly affects the reproduction of the workforce), the inflation of the prices of raw materials and foodstuffs (especially agricultural, mineral and energetic), the staples of general consumption today, follows these speculative movements of big fictitious capital as it searches for secure, attractive and profitable conditions to protect its class interests. Thus, according to ECLAC, the price index of foodstuffs increased around 30 percent between June and December 2010, peaking in January 2011; between June and December 2010, the price of wheat was 94 percent and that of corn was 64 percent, while the prices of minerals and energy were increased even more.[62]

Official data from the Mexican Secretariat of Finance and Public Credit (SHCP) reveals that in Mexico, with a GDP of US$1.2 trillion in 2011, the prices of staple foods consumed by the majority of the population in May grew around twice the general average, at a rate of 6.25 percent in the previous 12 months.[63] The issue has obviously had a negative impact on household consumption, pushing up the cost of the monthly food bill that (partially) makes up the value of labour power and which, in the context of salary reductions, implies greater rates of exploitation in so far as the worker is forced to double her or his workday, to reduce her or his consumption, or even both. We can describe this process over a longer period:

60 Chris Harman, "Economic Crisis: Capitalism Exposed," *Socialist Review*, February 2008, accessed 20 October 2014, https://www.marxists.org/archive/harman/2008/02/crisis2.htm.
61 Xavier Vence, "Da burbulla financiero-alimentaria ás novas burbullas especulativas da enerxía e dos alimentos," in *Cadernos de formación* (Galicia: CIG, Fesga, 2008).
62 ECLAC, "Commodity Price Rises and Volatility Pose a Challenge to Latin American Economies" (press release), 21 May 2011, accessed 20 October 2014, http://www.cepal.org/cgi-bin/getProd.asp?xml=/prensa/noticias/comunicados/7/43527/P43527.xml&xsl=/prensa/tpl-i/p6f.xsl&base=/prensa/tpl/top-bottom.xslt.
63 "La débil actividad económica interna propició menor inflación," *La Jornada*, 10 June 2011, accessed 20 October 2014, http://www.jornada.unam.mx/2011/06/10/economia/029n1eco.

As in the case of other primary materials, the price of foodstuffs saw a rapid increase between 2006 and 2008, reaching its highest point of the last 30 years. Food groups that showed the strongest hikes were cereals (including rice), dairy products, oils and animal fats. Behind the financial crisis an important fall in prices was produced, followed by a tendency to spike which accelerated throughout 2010, registering a 50 percent increase. This situation led the FAO to issue an alert in January 2011, once the index rose above the established record in the summer of 2008.[64]

In terms of political economy, the driver of global inflation in the prices of primary and agricultural products is hegemonic fictitious-speculative capital over so-called 'futures pricing' (i.e., beyond the immediate future), a now privileged form of investment which, stimulated by the capitalist crisis, saw high rates of return in the 'commodity futures market in the 2004–2008 period' in Latin America.

Capitalist development can now be boiled down to a constant fight for profits, markets, and productivity gains, all of which have been institutionalised and normalised under neoliberalism. As we saw earlier in Chapter 1, *labour* and *capital*, while ontological and political spaces in bourgeois society, constitute the *antipodes* of the historical class society supported by the capitalist mode of production, whose dynamic influences other categories such as social class, culture, tradition, the formation of cities, language and the law. This statement is rooted in three theses put forward by Marx and by scientific Marxism regarding the philosophical, ontological conception of labour. First, labour is the primordial characteristic (*Urphänomen*) of humanity that defines social being.[65] Second, under capitalism, labour constitutes the *only factor* capable of producing value and, thus, surplus value. The quantity of the latter depends on the rate of profit and its derived forms, average and extraordinary. The less value incorporated in the productive process, the smaller the mass (and thus, the surplus value) appropriated by capital and the more the rate of profit is cut. And third, when capital abandons the sphere of production and enters that of circulation (in the market), it is unproductive; an automobile that is not sold provides no gain to the manufacturer. It is in this sense that,

64   Daniel Munevar, "Alzas en los precios de alimentos. Una mirada desde América Latina," *Documento de Discusión* 1, Comité pour l'Annulation de la Dette du Tiers Monde, June 2011, accessed 20 October 2014, http://www.rebelion.org/docs/131093.pdf.

65   György Lukács, *Ontology of the Social Being. Volume 3: Labour* (London: Merlin Press, 1980).

This realization process is at the same time the de-realization process of labour. It posits itself objectively, but it posits this, its objectivity, as its own not-being or as the being of its not-being—of capital.[66]

Capital leaves production and, at this moment, also refuses as a condition to enter circulation (the market) once again. But it needs to pass through the latter, the somewhat unproductive sphere of capital, as an *condition immanent* to being realised and to generating *new* value (self-valorisation). In this cyclical and pervasive movement, capital simultaneously displaces the workforce from industries, services, activities, territories, regions and countries of the world, to form entire surplus populations of workers (thus spurring migration), while capital is itself dislocated to speculative activities which are profitable, but which render capital, for periods at a time, from the sphere of material and subjective production of value. While it is true that more products will be created (use values, wealth) following an increase in labour productivity, increasingly less (exchange) value will be created over the long term; in this way, the tendency of capital shows signs of making "human labour (relatively) superfluous, so as to drive it, as human labour, towards infinity."[67] This contradiction, between labour's superfluity for capital and the latter's need to exploit the former to obtain surplus value and profits, is the essence of the capitalist mode of production. The outcome is that capital ends up cutting the rate of surplus value and, through competition, distribution and private appropriation, of profit; these are interlinked phenomena that lead the system into further crisis.

In keeping with Marx, when capital is concentrated in the financial sphere (in banks, stock exchanges, trade, circulation) it depreciates. Capital is capable of creating neither value nor surplus value in these spheres, but rather only in the spheres of production and the labour process: the socially-necessary space-time where labour power combines with the means of production and with the transformation of nature to produce the means of consumption and new means of production which then revitalise the process of reproduction of capital on a greater scale. In this way,

> ...devaluation forms one moment of the realization process; which is already simply implied in the fact that the product of the process in its immediate form is not *value*, but first has to enter anew into circulation in order to be realized as such. Therefore, while capital is reproduced as value and new value in the production process, it is at the same time

---

66   Marx, *Grundrisse*, 454.
67   Marx, *Grundrisse*, 399.

posited as *not-value*, as something which first has to be *realized as value by means of exchange.*[68]

According to Marx, the valorisation/devalorisation process includes both the conservation of value (in the means of production, instruments, and labour power) as well as the creation of surplus value and thus requires both spheres (production, circulation). As Mészáros writes,

> Capital as a historically specific value-producing potential cannot be actualized and 'realized' (and through its 'realization' simultaneously also reproduced in an extended form) without entering the domain of *circulation*. The relationship between *production* and *consumption* is thus radically redefined within its framework in such a way that the much needed unity of the two becomes insuperably problematical, bringing with it as time goes by also the necessity of crises in one form or another.[69]

This contradiction between production and circulation, between supply and consumption, explains capital's need to develop modern marketing methods and to generate forms of realisation of the commodity that effectively shrink the distance between spheres; for example, the (originally Japanese) *just in time* system that supposedly gives priority to the vagaries of consumer demand and the 'overdetermination' of production. Moreover, this inherent dependency on capital circulation is one of the particularities distinguishing capitalism as a mode of production from prior social and productive formations which did not depend on exchange value for survival, and instead on use values as central elements of consumption and social reproduction produced in a given community. This speaks to the peculiar characteristic of bourgeois society, supported by the capitalist mode of production that in modern life unleashes,

> ...in an untiring, repetitive manner a mechanism that systematically subordinates the 'logic of use value,' the spontaneous sense of concrete life, of labour and human enjoyment, of production and consumption of 'earthly goods,' to the abstract 'logic' of 'value' as a substance that is blind and indifferent to all concreteness, and which only needs a profit margin to be validated as an 'exchange value.' It is the implacable reality of alienation, of the submission of the human will to the hegemony of

---

68   Marx, *Grundrisse*, 403.
69   Meszaros, *Beyond Capital*, 46.

the purely materialised 'will' of the world of commodities inhabited by capitalist economic value.[70]

On the other hand,

> ...what is specific to capitalism are therefore three things: a) the dynamic and unlimited character of investment and reinvestment processes, a mechanism that loops time and again, and generally without any kind of political barrier or historical limits; b) the incursion of capital in the sphere of production (the foundation of manufacturing and industry, industrial work performed in the home, etc.), not simply in the sphere of commerce (purchases of products wholesale in order to resell for greater profit); and, c) the existence of workers disposed or forced to become waged workers. Only when these three preconditions are in place, a situation which did not occur prior to the 17th century, does the economy stop being the means for reaching certain (social, cultural) objectives and become an end or goal in itself, capable of generating a powerful, irrepressible social dynamism. Only then can we speak of capitalism.[71]

This set of specific characteristics that we associate with capitalism, and which converge in the problems of overproduction and realisation of commodities, constantly generate difficulties for the production of value and surplus value under the goal of expanded reproduction. It is the latter that allows the cyclical continuity of money capital, productive capital and commodity capital, as well as the concentration and centralisation which drives the development of fictitious capital. It has likewise enabled the contraction of average rates of growth in production and the economy more generally, which has plunged capitalism into the most severe crisis, and led to a tumultuous situation in which the dominant theoretical apparatus is rendered useless.

Throughout history, capital has deployed processes to recover the rate of profit in order to secure its own reproduction. We are reminded of the factors of recovery of capitalist profitability that Marx described in *Capital*:

1.   The increase in the intensity of labour exploitation.
2.   The reduction of wages below their value (super-exploitation).

---

70   Bolívar Echeverría, *Valor de uso y utopía* – 2nd edition (Ciudad de México: Siglo XXI Editores, 2010), 63.
71   Fernández, *Clase*, 118.

3. The cheapening of the elements of constant capital (machinery, primary materials, building structures).

4. The increase of unemployment and underemployment following, amongst other things, the reduction of personnel employed by firms (downsizing).

5. The expansion of trade in the global market.

6. The crease of capital shares (fictitious capital).[72]

These mechanisms, typically used to counteract the fall of the rate of profit, have not only remained in play, but now are expanding with no end in sight in conjunction with newer mechanisms. These include the spectacular development of new forms of speculative finance capital (fictitious capital); the transnational strategies of multinational firms; the generalisation and universalisation of labour super-exploitation and the law of value (globalisation); the use of new methods of production and labour organisation through information systems and technological development. They also involve the shape given to public policies to benefit the general profitability and expansion of capital by the neoliberal state, as evident today in European countries where the State (as the guardian of the social metabolism of capital) guarantees the connection between the production of surplus value and its control as well as the structural hierarchical division of labour.[73]

The central element of this new morphology of social relations (i.e., of production and of the organisation of labour, including Toyotism and flexible automatisation) is the rationalisation of capital towards the goal of appropriating the subjectivity of labour (knowledge and wisdom of workers) to intensify the labour process.[74] As well identified by Sadi Dal Rosso, Toyotism is a system that elevates the level of labour intensity to a degree achieved by no other historical process.[75]

Keeping in mind the limits imposed under Taylorism and Fordism to the capacity of the capitalist to appropriate the knowledge of the collective worker, Toyotism by contrast places special emphasis on the effort to subordinate, codify and systematise workers' knowledge in order to produce value and surplus value. Scientific knowledge incorporated in the labour process, as well as the complexity of machinery following the development of

72   Marx, *Capital – Volume III*, Chapter 14.
73   Mészáros, *Beyond Capital*, 53.
74   For more on the theme of Toyotism and its relation to the subjectivity of the worker, see Antunes, *The Meanings of Work*, Chapter 4.
75   Dal Rosso, *Mais Trabalho*, 69.

information systems that reduce (or nullify) the control and understanding the worker has over it, contributes to this new command over labour. Instead of destroying workers' knowledge and skill set (as occurred previously under Tayorism and Fordism),[76] Toyotism not only deskills professionals, eroding their autonomy, organisation and decision-making power, but it also transforms them into "pluri-employed workers, into polyvalent professionals, into multifunctional workers"[77] which, bowing before the power of business, significantly enhances their levels of productivity. Labour intensity is also prioritised by attention to eliminating gaps in production and the working day, which effectively represent moments of anti-value in that they do not see the production of surplus value.

Since the 1980s, both procedures, part of the Toyotist system of production and organisation of labour, have been directed towards overcoming the crisis of labour time and the dismeasure of value that it implies as key elements of the modern social metabolism of capital. The *just in time* system, work teams, total quality control circles, and the *Kan Ban* system are just a few mechanisms associated with the new pattern of flexible accumulation. Before the crisis, the imposition of productive restructuring was needed to institute the more pernicious elements of the Toyotist system while, at the same time, generalizing the regime of super-exploitation, particularly in the economies and productive processes of central countries like the United States, Germany, and Japan, to mention the most important.

In this respect, Arriola and Vasapollo characterise the new capitalist organisation of labour as being,

> ...increasingly marked by precariousness, flexibility, deregulation. It is a social situation marked by social unease at work for fear of losing one's very job, by virtue of not being able to ever develop a social life, and of pledging one's life only in and for work with the always present anxiety linked to the consciousness of a technological evolution that does not meeting social needs. It is a process that makes all of social living precarious.[78]

---

76 See Harry Braverman, *Labor and Monopoly Capitalism* (New York: Monthly Review, 1974).

77 Benjamín Coriat, *Pensar al revés. Trabajo y organización de la empresa japonesa* (Ciudad de México: Siglo XXI Editores, 1992), 41.

78 Joaquín Arriola and Luciano Vasapollo, *Flexibles y precarios. La opresión del trabajo en el nuevo capitalismo europeo* (Madrid: El Viejo Topo, 2003).

This is the profile of 21st century capitalism that is unfolding on a global scale; an unfolding which has included the intensive and systematic exploitation of natural resources in its processes of valorisation, putting them at the service of accumulation. Thus, we call this system authentically *toxic capitalism*, more so for its implication in the destructiveness of the human being. This has been accompanied by the revolutionary development of information technology and electronic means of communication, together with a series of practices and policies such as labour reform (which, for example, is meant to increase the working week of the European Union to 65 hours a week), the shrinking of real salaries already being observed in diverse sectors and productive branches, increased unemployment swelled by the crisis, the destruction of combative unionism, which has been unable to recover from the strong political and repressive attacks by the neoliberal state, and the development of business unions with a collaborationist bent (such as in Japan and the United States) resulting in the defeat of workers virtually everywhere.

Conclusion

The crisis of labour time, derived from the very development of the productive forces of society and the unceasing growth of labour productivity, has made it so that surplus labour and the production of surplus value have become increasing insufficient to mitigate the crisis and to buttress capital accumulation on an ever expanding scale, so as to guarantee, first, a recovery of the average rate of profit at a global level and, subsequently, reasonable profit levels for individual capitals by firm, branch and sector. It is this which is the most accurate measure of the development and 'health' of the system, regardless of what private and public policies are in place and it is on this measure that the remaining coordinates of the system and society *depends*: employment, salaries, public and social spending, industrial policies, credit and banking policy, and programmes for the social development of the population.

PART 2

The World of Work in the 21st Century

∴

CHAPTER 4

Surplus Value and the Super-exploitation of Labour

> The worker does not necessarily gain when the
> capitalist gains, but he necessarily loses with him. For
> example, the worker does not gain if the capitalist
> keeps the market price above the natural price
> by means of a manufacturing or trade secret, a
> monopoly or a favourably placed property.
>
> KARL MARX, *Economic and Philosophical Manuscripts of 1844, p. 283.*

Introduction

In the current chapter we will briefly present the theory of labour exploitation in
the context of Marx's political economy, particularly in his monumental works
The Grundrisse and *Capital*, for the purpose of establishing that this category has
an essential role to play in explaining the structure of the current capitalist crisis,
beginning with a series of interconnected phenomenon which have unleashed a
period of deficit throughout the system in terms of the production of value and
surplus value. In this setting, financial difficulties are only a reflection of the
underlying problem. We suggest that this crisis can only be overcome by resorting to an increase in the average rate of labour exploitation in classical terms and,
ultimately, to a *super-exploitation* of labour throughout the system, including
even the countries and productive systems of advanced capitalism.

Exploitation and the Labour Theory of Value

The theory of wage labour exploitation (central both to the monumental work
Capital and to *The Grundrisse*) has been constructed at a very high level of
abstraction. In this setting, the concept of exploitation (as a basic relational
and constituent category of historical capitalist society) is essential to the
theory of surplus value and profit within the capitalist mode of production,
and in no other, be it feudal or servile. Without such a concept, the development and understanding of the labour theory of value as the central axis of
capitalist production and reproduction is inconceivable.

The conception of labour as an ontological, historical and social category, and the central place that it occupies in capitalist society, sets the thought of Marx and Engels' apart from all previous philosophical elaborations (from Aristotle to Hegel), and from those which have followed (positivism, structuralism and postmodernism). Today, of course, it also provides a point of contrast to neoclassical economics, neo-Keynesianism, and neo-structural social sciences, as well as to metaphysical conceptions of the 'end of work' thesis, all of which have attempted to reintroduce positivism in theoretical formulations which purport to 'account' for post-industrial society.

According to Lukács, this distinctiveness stems from the fact that Marx conceives all teleology as human praxis towards a given end, based on labour as the foundation of material reality rather than external to it.[1] Other currents— including those that see labour as one 'factor of production' amongst so many others, or as an 'accessory,' complementary or declining factor, and finally, those that subordinate it to categories such as technology, science and employment (the evolutionary school)—are unfortunately all deeply rooted in the sociology, economics and anthropology of phenomena such as the exploitation of the workforce, private ownership over the means of production and consumption, the expropriation and pauperisation of the consumption fund of workers and of nations; phenomena which are taken to be an 'optical illusion' by those who refuse to 'recognise' the advantages and benefits of capitalist globalisation which has ultimately brought about 'justice' for so many.

The labour theory of value positions the methods of exploitation that we identified earlier (absolute and relative surplus value) as central to the reproduction of the system over the long term, whereby the means of production (in conjunction with labour power) is limited to transferring and conserving its own value, as set forth in Chapter 2. This presupposes an understanding of both forms of surplus value as concepts grounded in specific socio-historical formations in which labour processes and social relations of production interact. As Marini suggests:

> ...capitalist production, by developing the productive force of labour, does not eliminate but rather deepens the exploitation of the worker; and secondly, that the forms of capitalist exploitation are combined unequally throughout the system as a whole, giving shape to distinct social formations under the dominance of a particular form.[2]

---

1 Lukács, *Ontology,* 8.
2 Marini, *Dialéctica,* 93.

A periodisation of historical development on the grounds of these two conceptions of surplus value (amongst others) will need to consider the predominance (or lack) of labour productivity on the basis of technological development over the extension of the working day and intensification of labour, or their combination, using these to set benchmarks in the study of the development of the capitalist mode of production. While in Europe, the transition from feudalism to capitalism was marked by the industrial revolution and the rise of big industry, in Latin America, this transition would be marked by the rise of an export economy under the land-owning oligarchy and, following the Second World War, the flourishing of the nation-state model of industrialisation based on the substitution of imports for the internal market.[3]

From another vantage point, this so-called transition marks the boundary between the development of absolute surplus value and the growing hegemony of relative surplus value as the central category of capital accumulation and valorisation. Regarding this periodisation, Marini writes,

> The export-oriented economy constitutes the stage of transition to a genuinely national capitalist economy which only took shape with the emergence of the industrial economy...the survivals of older modes of production which prevailed in the colonial economy still determine the manner in which the laws of dependent capitalist development manifest to a considerable degree. The significance of the regime of slave production in the determination of the current economy in certain Latin American countries, like Brazil, is fact that cannot be avoided.[4]

It should be noted that, in general, historical capitalism has always been confronted with pre-capitalist social relations and production, which does not undermine the related point that it is capitalism (as a mode of production) that shapes the way in which economic, social and political structures interact. In other words, as Marini suggests, "capitalism represents the core of the analysis...where capitalist property is and will always be a particular form of private property."[5] The conclusion reached in the specific case above is that the modes

---

3 For Michel Chossudovsky, *The Globalisation of Poverty: impacts of IMF and World Bank Reforms* (London: Zed Books, 1999), the concepts of "import substitution and production for the internal market" are now obsolete, replaced by a specialised pattern of capitalist reproduction in primary production for the global market (77).

4 Marini, *Dialéctica*, 82–3.

5 Ruy Mauro Marini, "Introducción: la década de 1970 revisitada," in *La teoría social latinoamericana. Volume III, La centralidad del marxismo*, edited by Ruy Mauro Marini and Márgara Millán (Ciudad de México: El Caballito, 1995), 10.

of production (slavery, serfdom) dating from the colonial period, which were later subsumed under the economic and political hegemony of dependent capitalism, determine to some degree the particular manner in which the general laws of capitalism (in particular, the super-exploitation of labour) came to operate, in keeping with the historical and structural specificities of the socio-economic and political formation in question.

One of these structural determinants of the dependent economy consists of the fact that earlier structures of production constitute obstacles to the emergence of a regime of capitalist accumulation under the hegemony of relative surplus value, contrary to what occurred during 'classical capitalism.' The repercussions of this have lasted until the present day. In effect,

> ...precapitalist structures, while combined and integrated under the domination of the capitalist mode of production, are objects of a slow process of absorption; whereas, in conditions of dependency, the same capitalist mode of production encounters difficulties in the effort to generalize relative surplus value, and so, the tendency to establish extraordinary surplus value is hindered (which is expressed in obstacles to the levelling out of the rate of profit).[6]

As we will see below, this initial challenge, and the subsequent slowness with which relative surplus value became generalised in the dependent economy, its systems of production and work, constitute weaknesses that explain the problems of underdevelopment and backwardness which affect the region to this day, including in developing countries which are relatively more advanced like Brazil, Argentina and Mexico.

Marini's Approach to the Sociology of Work

Marini contributed important theoretical and analytical tools to the sociology of labour in order to aid in the understanding of global phenomena from a perspective that is both critical and grounded in the socio-economic formations of dependent economies (in particular, those of Latin America) as a whole, which differed from the trajectories of historical development of European capitalism. Specifically, he pointed to the necessary *articulation* of (absolute and relative) surplus value with the development of labour productivity, and

---

6   Ruy Mauro Marini, "Estado y crisis en Brasil," *Cuadernos Políticos* (Ciudad de México) 13 (July-September 1977): 76.

so, with technology in the context of expanding global capitalism by means of the integration of dependent and underdeveloped countries and their subordination to the economies of the hegemonic centres.

From this point of departure, the following points emerge: first, from their very beginning, these countries historically helped to hasten the transition from absolute to relative surplus value in the developed countries of classical capitalism (particularly England), specifically during the industrial revolution. Second, dependent countries, regardless of their 'degree of development' (i.e., even those, like Brazil, which belong to the select group of BRICS) continue to transfer value and surplus value to hegemonic capitalist countries under the rubric of *unequal exchange*; in this context, labour super-exploitation is provoked, if not directly driven, by such exchange, as Marini clarifies here:

> The superexploitation of labour is spurred by unequal exchange, but it does not derive from it; rather, it derives from the fever for profits created by the global market and based fundamentally on the formation of a relative super-population. But, once an economic process on the basis of superexploitation is underway, it sets in motion a monstrous mechanism whose perversity, far from abating, is accentuated as the dependent economy resorts to increases of productivity through technological development.[7]

---

7 Marini, "Las razones," 63–4. It is useful to recall the *original* discussion on unequal exchange between Arghiri Emmanuel, Charles Bettelheim and Samir Amin, although it appeared to have little impact (at least directly) on the discussions in Latin America; in particular, in the development of dependency theory. Emmanuel was one of the first to shift from the theory of comparative costs of international trade based on the analysis of price, to study unequal exchange between nations starting from the exchange of unequal quantities of labour to the detriment of underdeveloped countries. Thus, his question, "Is there, for certain reasons that the dogma of immobility of factors prevents us from seeing, a certain category of countries that, whatever they undertake and whatever the produce, always exchange a larger amount of their national labor for a smaller amount of foreign labor?" He responds in the affirmative, and on that basis, develops his theory of unequal exchange. Arghiri Emmanuel, *Unequal Exchange: a study of the imperialism of trade,* translated by Brian Pearce (London: Monthly Review, 1972), xxxi. The debate over unequal exchange appears in Arghiri Emmanuel, et al., "Imperialismo y comercio desigual" (special issue) *Cuadernos de Pasado y Presente 24* (Córdoba), 1971. It should be mentioned that, in the work of Marini, no reference to this discussion is made. For him, ECLAC alone (particularly in the figure of Prebisch) developed a theory of the 'deteriorating terms of trade,' which evades the important issue of value transfers and the prices of production which operate at the level of the market. As such, Magnus Blomström and Björn Hettne, in *La teoría del desarrollo en transición* (Ciudad de México: Fondo de Cultura Económia, 1990), suggest that "The development of a theory of unequal exchange was not, then, linked directly to the Latin American dependency school, even while various Latin American authors were working on the same theme" (107).

TABLE 7 *Surplus value extraction in developed and dependent capitalist countries*

Developed capitalist countries	Dependent capitalist countries
Labour productivity (relative surplus value)	Super-exploitation (combination of absolute surplus value, intensity of the labour process, and expropriation of the consumption fund of the workforce)
Vlp = sv (wages)	Vlp > sv (wages)

Finally (and somewhat contradictorily), dependent countries have helped to block or discourage the development of relative surplus value on the basis of labour productivity within the very heart of capitalist systems of production and reproduction, tending to deepen even further labour super-exploitation starting from the reduction of the consumption fund of workers, which is converted it into an additional source of capital accumulation.

On the other hand, we note two *typologies* in *Dialéctica de la dependencia* that underpin the thesis of dependency and labour super-exploitation.

As we can see in Table 7, prior to the industrialisation of the Latin American countries (1850–1945), labour super-exploitation was "a mode of production founded exclusively on the greater exploitation of the worker, and not on the development is her or his productive capacity,"[8] as occurred in the industrialised countries where, *grosso modo*, the price of the worker's labour power (in principle) corresponded to its value, which did not occur in dependent economies.[9] Obviously, these differentiated modes of production would have a distinct effect on the consumption of workers. In effect,

> Far from a mode of development which, on the basis of increased labour productivity, integrates growing segments of the population to consumption, what prevails in a dependent economy like that of Brazil

---

8   Marini, *Dialéctica*, 40.

9   In the theoretical and methodological development of *Capital*, Marx presupposes that the value of commodities and of labour power correspond to their prices. In this respect, he tells us that, "We started with the supposition that labour-power is bought and sold at its value. Its value, like that of all other commodities, is determined by the working-time necessary to its production." Marx, *Capital – Volume I*, 231. Another section reminds us that, "we have assumed that commodities are bought and sold at their values...." Marx, *Capital – Volume II*, 132.

are forms of labour superexploitation (themselves sharpened by increasing rates of productivity), which not only exclude these masses from consumption, but which do so also from productive employment created by the accumulation of capital.[10]

In the general outline of Latin American industrialisation,[11] the development of the productive forces and subsequent increased rates of labour productivity (relative surplus value) also lent to the consolidation of the regime of super-exploitation combining both absolute surplus value (prolongation of the working day, or line c-d in Table 4) and relative surplus value (intensification and the lowering of necessary labour time, or line a-b in Table 3) with the *expropriation* of part of the necessary labour of the worker. Together, this gave rise to a specific form of capitalist accumulation and exploitation of the workforce which, as a whole, causes the rates of surplus value (sv/v) and of profit (sv/c+v) to rise simultaneously.[12] In practice, this *regime* gives rise to a specific mode of labour exploitation that generates a *cycle of dependent capitalism sui generis* in which the functioning and reproduction of the dependent economy is subordinated to the international economy; in particular, to the hegemonic cycles of imperialist countries.[13]

TABLE 8   *The super-exploitation of labour*

a - - - b - - - - c = 8 hours
a - - - b - - - - c = 8 hours
a - - b - - - - - - c = 8 hours
a - b - - - - - - - c = 8 hours

---

10   Ruy Mauro Marini, *Subdesarrollo y revolución – 5ª edición* (Ciudad de México: Siglo XXI Editores, 1974), xi.

11   Particularly in the larger countries of the region, this involved a first period of "autonomous development" (1930–1950), and a second characterized by the "integration of the systems of production and subimperialism" (1960–1980). See Estela Gutiérrez Garza & Edgar González Gaudiano, *De las teorías del desarrollo al desarrollo sustentable* (Ciudad de México: Universidad Autónoma de Nuevo León, Siglo XXI Editores, 2010), 53.

12   Marini, *Dialéctica*, 41. "It is understood that in these circumstances, productive activity is based above all on the extensive and intensive use of labour power: this allows it to lower the value composition of capital which, coupled with the intensification of the degree of labour exploitation, makes it so that the rates of surplus value and of profit rise simultaneously."

13   Marini, *Dialéctica*, 42.

In Table 8, the line a-b corresponds to the value of labour power as reflected in the wage; it is reduced by the expropriating action of capital, modifying both magnitudes of the working day, even though the assumption is that neither the length nor the intensity of the working day increases. The expropriation of part of the consumption fund of the workers thus becomes an additional source of capital accumulation that benefits the rate of profit. In this sense,

> the concept of superexploitation seeks to *structurally* account for the peculiar development of capitalism in the periphery, for its dependent and integrated, unequal and combined, contradictory and fraught character, by way of two essential determinants: the truncation of the law of value, and the precariousness of the internal market.[14]

However, what is peculiar about this *regime* of labour super-exploitation is that it hinders the development of productive capacity both structurally and socially, and the possibility of incorporating cutting edge technology into labour processes; these phenomena prevent relative surplus value from becoming hegemonic and capable of leading the economic process of dependent countries, as occurred with the development of classical capitalism in advanced countries. In this regard, Marini points to the social characteristics and consequences of such a regime:

> ...in the three mechanisms under consideration, the key factor is given in the fact that the worker is denied the conditions necessary to replenish his or her spent labour power: in the first two cases (the intensity and prolongation of the working day), because he or she is forced to expend a greater degree of labour power than would be normally provided, thereby leading to his or her premature exhaustion; and the latter (the expropriation of the workers consumption fund), because it removes even the possibility of consuming what is strictly speaking indispensible to conserve his or her labour power under normal circumstances. In capitalist terms, these mechanisms (which, moreover, may occur in combinations, and usually do) signify that labour is remunerated below its value, and so, corresponds to a superexploitation of labour.[15]

Super-exploitation does not operate in a vacuum, or as an 'autarkic,' 'autonomous economic mechanism,' without being mediated and indeed overdetermined

---

14   Fontes, *O capital-imperialismo*, 352.
15   Marini, *Dialéctica*, 41–2.

by class, political and cultural structures, contrary to the superficial charges levelled at the main approaches of dependency theory by its critics. To the contrary, it is a complete, fully functioning and multifaceted system, structural in nature but also requiring State participation and political power (including through recourse to repression) to ensure its effective operation as both an economic and social formation. Once established (towards the end of the 19th century cycle of independence which forged the dependent, underdeveloped nation states of Latin America), labour super-exploitation helped to reproduce historical and structural dependency, forging its own cycle within the dependent economy. As Marini indicated in relation to the first moment of dependency (in the context of the so-called export economy),

> In dependent countries, the sphere of production is tightly linked to the circulation of money capital and merchant capital (under the form of the means of production), originating from the advanced capitalist countries.[16]

But, he continues, in the second stage (Latin American industrialisation), "...in any scenario, this flow, once internalised, is a determining factor in shaping the economic cycle of the dependent countries." It thus constitutes a separate but dependent cycle, which necessarily is reproduced in keeping with international variables and the predominance of the mode of production of the hegemonic centres. Marini's approach in this regard is as follows:

> Breaking therefore from the mode of circulation that characterised the export economy, the dependent industrial economy reproduces, in a particular way, capital accumulation based on the super-exploitation of the worker. Consequently, it also reproduces a mode of circulation corresponding to this kind of accumulation, albeit in a modified form: it is no longer the dissociation between the production and circulation of commodities as a function of the global market at work, but rather the separation between the high and low spheres of circulation within the economy itself; a separation which, rather than being offset by factors at work in the classical capitalist economy, acquires a much more radical character.[17]

For her part, Vania Bambirra explains the inner workings of the dependent economy in terms of how its operation is structured more generally: in the

---

16   Marini, "Estado," 79.

17   Marini, *Dialéctica*, 63–4.

export economy, both sector I (which produces means of production) and sector II (producing the means of consumption) were located in the exterior. Later, industrialisation saw the internal development of sector II, but only in countries like Mexico or Brazil. However, the same did not take place with sector I, which resulted in the massive importation of machinery and other industrial inputs. Beginning from the 1950s with the rise of Latin American developmentalist theories,[18] sector I began to be established in Latin America, but without breaking from dependency on foreign direct investment and transnational corporations. It is this, according to Bambirra, which accounts for the specificity of the cycle of capital in dependent economies:

> ...capital accumulation passes through the exterior with the importation of machinery; once machinery begins to be produced internally (only in certain countries and with many limitations in advanced technology sectors like electronics and nuclear energy, which are monopolised by the more developed countries), it is still controlled directly by foreign groups. Even when the dependent economy begins to meet the needs for machinery in sector II (which certainly also ends up being controlled to a large degree by foreign capital), it remains dependent on the technology-capital of sector I of the developed capitalist countries.[19]

The dependent economy thus entered a vicious cycle from which it has proven incapable of escaping in as much as it never completed its own cycle of industrialisation; and moreover, due to the fact that there are still obstacles preventing this completion deriving as much from the form that industrialisation (albeit truncated, incomplete and insufficient) has taken as to the manner in which the capitalist cycle articulates with the structures of class and political power in the dependent social formations of Latin America.

Two Patterns of Capital Accumulation: Structural Heterogeneity vs. Technological Standardisation

The international economy has entered a phase characterised by the progressive dismantling of national economic frontiers (globalisation) aimed at

---

18   In this respect, see the work of Fernando Fajnzylber, *La industrialización trunca en América Latina – 4th edition* (Ciudad de México: Nueva Imagen, 1988); "Industrialización en América Latina. De la 'caja negra' al 'casillero vacío,'" *Cuadernos de la CEPAL 60* (Santiago de Chile: Naciones Unidas, 1990).

19   Vania Bambirra, *Teoría de la dependencia: una anticrítica* (Ciudad de México: Era, 1978).

reaching increasingly broader, particular, complex and competitive markets and, thereby, gradually intensifying the competition between global multinationals to make (and appropriate) extraordinary profits, which are the contemporary motor of capitalist development.[20] In this context, technological diffusion has spread in the effort to standardise commodities and to facilitate their exchange on a global scale, provoking a marked tendency over the long term towards the standardisation of productive processes, productivity and, at the same time, the intensification of labour. This process has largely contributed to standardising work, productive and exploitative conditions of labour in capitalist countries, and to restricting differences from emerging in the organisation of the labour process (particularly between developed and dependent countries). Speaking to this latter point, Hirata establishes that

> [i]n technological terms, there is little difference between parent establishments and their affiliates, since multinationals aim to make the same product in every country. In order to do so, they need advanced technology. Moreover, since the 1980s, globalisation has enabled the wide circulation of commodities throughout the world, requiring the need to formalize a standard of quality for international competitivity; something that would be difficult to guarantee if one were to depend on obsolete machinery or materials. While there is not much difference in terms of technology, the problem is that advances take place quickly in the centre (in France and Japan), and much more slowly in countries like Brazil. After five years the delay is apparent in the Third World.... It is in the organisation of labour where the greatest differences are noticeable.[21]

Similarly, Rifkin argues that since it is no longer possible to compete in global markets with old-fashioned factories organised around intensive labour, the traditional division that existed between the developed North (home to advanced technology) and the South (with its cheap labour and obsolete technologies) no longer works. Now the latest technology, optimal quality controls, productive systems based on *just in time* supply chains and adequate stock to reduce the risk of overproduction and backed up stockrooms are all necessary. His argument is based on the fact that the cheapest worker

---

20   Ruy Mauro Marini, "Proceso y tendencias de la globalización capitalista," in *La teoría social latinoamericana. Volume IV, Cuestiones contemporáneas,* edited by Ruy Mauro Marini and Márgara Millán (Ciudad de México: El Caballito, 1996), 49–68.

21   Helena Hirata, "¿Sociedad del ocio? El trabajo se intensificó" (interview), *Página 12* (Buenos Aires), 2 January 2001, accessed 23 November 2014, http://www.pagina12.com .ar/2001/01-02/01-02-12/pag11.htm.

in the world no longer costs as much as the online technology that replaces him or her:

> Business leaders throughout the world have said to me that the technology they're producing is so cheap they can give it away.... They use it as an introduction to their clients and what it does is to co-manage their business.[22]

This is clearly illustrated in the various stages of the maquiladora industry in Mexico which has passed from simple assembly to the introduction of *just in time* production and, more recently, to automated lines which generate highly-skilled technical jobs. Specialised labour processes have also arisen in design and research and development linked to transnational corporations.[23]

The growing standardisation of technology and its diffusion the world over has also lead to the levelling of prices and to the generalisation of the law of value, since:

> ...the remarkable progress made by information and communications technology has provided a much more solid basis for knowing the conditions of production, and therefore, for establishing relative prices. In more highly integrated productive sectors, the global market is moving in the direction of levelling (ever more effectively) values and has *tended* to eliminate national differences that affect the validity of the law of value.[24]

Contributing to this dramatic opening of nations and global markets beginning in the 1980s were the economic and political practices associated with neoliberalism: external opening, the privatisation of the public sector, financial liberalisation, the dismantling of the social institutions of the welfare state, and the regulation of the workforce, employment and wages by market forces and extraordinary rates of profit. Rather than leading to the strengthening of national economies (through greater autonomy in global markets and internal decision-making capacity around issues of national sovereignty within an international framework based upon symmetric relations)

---

22   Jeremy Rifkin, "Tiempo libre para disfrutarlo o hacer filas de desempleados," in *Un mundo sin trabajo,* edited by Luis Álvarez (Ciudad de México: Díada, 2003), 15–49.

23   See David Ibarra, *Ensayos sobre economía mexicana* (Ciudad de México: Fondo de Cultural Económica, 2005), 268.

24   Marini, "Proceso," 64 (italics in the original).

this process has, instead, led to the constitution of dependent neoliberal economies exposed and subordinated to the economic cycles of the hegemonic countries of advanced capitalism.[25]

Labour Power: Strategic to the Production of Extraordinary Profits

Contrary to the conjectures of the 'end of work' thesis, labour power remains essential for the accumulation and reproduction of capital in globalised capitalism. In this sense, it lies at the heart of neoliberal policies driving the restructuring of production and labour processes that are now being implemented in the European Union: those which require the worker to perform *additional toil without salary compensation*, and those which snatch part of her or his fund of consumption and reproduction, whether by delaying the age of retirement, privatising the health and education system, or by raising taxes which hurt his or her purchasing power and consumption. In this context, speaking of the end of labour sounds ridiculous,

> All the more with the gradual cancellation of the social pacts of the Fordist era, the actual workweek tending to stretch in recent years, when the tendency is to delay the age of retirement, and when work or study directly related to work (the preparation of reports, crash seminars, tax returns) tends to increasingly take over the hours of the weekend and vacation time.[26]

The tendency of different organic compositions of capital in the global economy and the process of technological standardisation to equalise has in fact increased the importance of the worker as the *source of extraordinary profit*. Hence, labour super-exploitation has been made central to the effort to confront the sharpening of global capitalist competition, and to counter difficulties faced by capital in the production of value and surplus value. In this sense, the new

---

25   It may be argued that even Brazil, which exhibits a level of capitalist development and political autonomy adequate to see it included as a member of the BRICS, has nonetheless maintained its condition as peripheral to and subordinated by advanced countries of hegemonic capitalism; something that Ruy Mauro Marini accounted for with the concept of *subimperialism*. In this respect, see Virgínia Fontes, *O capital-imperialismo*, and Mathias Luce, "La expansión del subimperialismo brasileño," *Rebelión*, 12 April 2008, accessed 23 November 2014, http://www.rebelion.org/noticia.php?id=76977.

26   Fernández, *Clase*, 21–2.

organisation of labour (Toyotism and other flexible devices corresponding to neo-Fordism) should be understood as part of an effort to intensify the exploitation of labour power and to break its resistance to such changes; and therefore, to reassess the worker as the source of value production and competitivity.

Globalisation generalises and stimulates the extension of the law of value, determining the value of labour power and of (material and immaterial) commodities by means of the socially-necessary labour time for their production (and in the case of labour power, reproduction) in truly international conditions. With the help of network technology, it is now easier to determine the value of the labour power of Japanese, German, North American or Mexican workers, and to measure its quantitative and qualitative magnitudes.

Moreover, globalisation so defined extends not only to the workforce, but also to other elements that determine the cost of production, including fixed capital (which includes the means of production and instruments of labour) and land (understood here as a means of production, but also as a means of circulation, as raw material that is incorporated in the final product, the commodity). What these three elements (labour power, land, and capital) have in common is that globalisation simultaneously has spread technical progress through the incorporation of leading technology into productive processes: information technology, biotechnology, the materials and microelectronics associated with fourth generation computers, characterised by the production of electronics integrated by interactive cybernetic networks.[27] Technologies designed by the transnational centres of the dominant scientific and technological capitals to develop a qualitatively distinct, superior industrial and organisational paradigm, one which, *grosso modo*, was recognised in the past as Fordism/Taylorism and which energised industrial production throughout the post-war period.

The Precariousness of the World of Work

We would like to devote a few words to the precarisation of labour, which is such a sign of our times that many authors and social movements have characterised movements of the working classes angled against the neoliberal policies, the globalisation of capital, and deterioration of working and living conditions in countries of the European Union as the *social precariat*. Alves

---

27   Giovanni Alves, *Dimensões da reestruturação produtiva. Ensaios de sociologia do trabalho* (São Paulo: Editora Praxis, 2007), 58.

distinguishes the concept of *precariousness* from that of *precarisation*.[28] While the former is an *inherent condition* of wage labour, the latter corresponds to the *process* of redeploying this condition in a new way. Thus, the precarisation of labour in the context of capital globalisation is associated with new economic trends that "...express the contradictions of recent productive transformations at an international level."[29] For this author, the new conditions of precariousness have followed from the breakup of the alliance between the 'market society' and welfare state, as well as the withdrawal of the latter from social provisioning in the areas of employment and social security.

Finally, it should be pointed out that in addition to these factors, at the centre of labour precariousness is a growing loss of social and labour rights for the worker, which have ended up affecting society more generally. Precariousness thus takes on a social dimension, as clearly illustrated here:

> This, then, is the centre of the problem and the centre of the conflict: it is about rendering from 'work' the right to have rights, and particularly, the right to what is produced and producible without labour, or increasingly less labour. It is about paying heed that no longer is the right to an income, to full citizenship, nor to the development and identity of all be centred around the occupation of a job, and to depend upon it. And consequently, it is about changing society.[30]

The precarisation of labour is making great strides the world over, reshaping countless professional categories. This has given rise to a new working class called the *precariat* which is now fighting to recover its rights and further its demands in Europe, the United States and Japan. A recent expression of this social phenomenon is the struggle taken up by youth and unions in the United States through Occupy Wall Street against the neoliberal policies of the government under the slogan, "We speak for the 99%—not the 1% that keep getting richer!"

In this context, we identify labour flexibilisation and precarisation as the most far-reaching transformations of the structural and institutional order of the past two decades. Placed in service of the needs of production, productivity and market dynamics, these trends have had a negative impact on wages, contractual categories and the functions performed by workers. They have also

---

28   Alves, *Dimensões*, 113 et seq.
29   Dídimo Castillo Fernández, *Los nuevos trabajadores precarios* (Ciudad de México: Miguel Ángel Porrúa, Universidad Autónoma del Estado de México, 2009), 39.
30   Gorz, *Miseria del presente*, 64.

seen an increase in the incident of work-related illness and deaths in their wake. In the 2011 edition of its annual *Death on the Job* report, the AFL-CIO highlighted the rising incidence of death in the workplace:

> In 2009, according to preliminary data from the Bureau of Labor Statistics, 4,340 workers were killed on the job—an average of 12 workers every day—and an estimated 50,000 died from occupational diseases. More than 4.1 million work-related injuries and illnesses were reported, but this number understates the problem. The true toll of job injuries is two to three times greater—about 8 million to 12 million job injuries and illnesses each year.[31]

On the other hand, the wave of suicides at France Telecom, which boasts 100,000 employees in France, tragically returned in the same period: between 2008 and 2010 there were more than 60 reported, of which 27 were linked to work, according to the union platform Observatory for Stress and Forced Labour Mobility.[32] A report by the International Labour Organisation revealed that around 6,300 people die each day globally due to work-related accident or illness (in other words, 2.3 million a year). 270 million workers suffer from work-related accidents and 160 million acquire occupational diseases; repetitive strain injury for example, is an occupational disease that occurs due to excessive repetitive strain over the course of a 14–15 hour workday, with little or no rest for the workers. Another associated phenomenon affecting the world of work is work-related stress (what psychologists have called burnout) that has been linked to at least three further conditions: emotional and physical exhaustion, low labour productivity, and chronic depersonalisation (a dissociative disorder).[33]

Hence, the super-exploitation and precariousness of labour, as socio-labour mechanisms of productive restructuring have been predicated on the deregulation of collective agreements, and their conversion into flexible, multipurpose devices that are easily adaptable to the needs of capital accumulation and valorisation, in the context of production and markets, with the express purpose of counteracting obstacles to the creation of value and surplus value experienced by capital in each productive cycle.

---

31   AFL-CIO, *Death on the Job: The Toll of Neglect – 20th edition* (Washington DC: American Federation of Labor& Congress of Industrial Organizations, 2011), 1.

32   Andrés Pérez, "La crisis de suicidios en France Telecom se reabre trágicamente," *Rebelion. org*, 28 April 2011, accessed 1 December 2014, http://www.rebelion.org/noticia.php?id =127314.

33   Sennett, *Corrosion*.

Conclusion

Super-exploitation is a category derived from the labour theory of value which expresses the specificity of social and productive relations at play in dependent social and economic formations. Marini contributed a theory of the specific nature of such societies using the tools provided by political economy, in particular, from *Capital*, which provides a general theory of the development, crisis, and decadence of capitalism.

We began by confirming the existence of two distinct social and economic formations in the global economy: one grounded in the greater extensive and intensive exploitation of the workforce, the other preferably in greater productivity. We then established that a strategy to standardise and disseminate technology by transnational corporations from advanced countries has spread to virtually all regions and countries since the 1980s, since which time the workforce has in fact become central to the production of extraordinary profits. In the context of the current global economic crisis, these countries have fully entered into a process of global competition to lower workers' salaries, increase the average length of the working day and, using methods of organising labour associated with Toyotism, intensified the use of labour with the aim of producing additional surplus value and compensating capital for the losses suffered under competition, and the tendency of the rate of profit to fall.

CHAPTER 5

The New Morphology of Capitalism

Introduction

This chapter aims to explore the premise that the super-exploitation of labour is becoming increasingly prevalent in the industrialised countries of a neurotic global capitalist system. Such a preliminary exercise will obviously not resolve the underlying issue, given the lack of empirical evidence that would be required to check our working hypothesis, particularly in relation to the most recent manifestations of the phenomenon. Nonetheless, the task is urgent and poses major theoretical and methodological challenges for Latin American dependency theory (the core issues thrown up by super-exploitation as an analytical concept having been initially synthesised in this context), particularly in the wake of capitalist globalisation and the significant economic, social, political and military transformations it entailed around the world, but particularly in Europe and the United States. At the same time, the centre-periphery relation has changed with the emergence of a new international division of labour that has come to benefit, to an extent, new imperialist subjects with hegemonic pretensions, like the republics of China and India.[1]

The Socio-political Significance of Old and New Peripheries in the Global Economy

Throughout the 1980s and 90s, capitalism and the global workforce underwent an international restructuring under the influence of a structural crisis which affected multiple regions and countries. Wages, job posts, and professional categories of work were forced to adjust to the macroeconomic and organisational conditions of the new regime of capitalist production and valorisation required by neoliberalism. In the United States, the wages and working conditions of workers and unions were affected by the transnational effects of the North

---

1   In this context, it is no wonder that the United States has, according to a 2008 report of the Pentagon, "865 installations in more than 40 countries...with more than 190 thousand soldiers deployed in more than 46 countries and territories." To these military bases, we should add the seven recently installed in Colombia, bringing the total to 872. Alfredo Jalife-Rahme, *El híbrido mundo multipolar. Un enfoque multidimensional* (Ciudad de México: Orfila, 2010), 38.

American Free Trade Agreement (NAFTA), imposed in 1994 by the governments and transnational corporations of the United States, Mexico and Canada; while in Europe, a similar social process took hold following the incorporation of ex-socialist countries of Eastern Europe in the productive systems (and exploitation) of western capitalism.

The incorporation of certain countries, the *new peripheries*, posed a great opportunity for corporations headquartered in the hegemonic capitalist countries of the European Union to take advantage of the former's 'competitive advantage', including lower wages, non-existent or weak unions, highly-qualified workforces and geographic proximity to fluid flows of raw materials and investments. Amongst other perks, these countries have presented big capital with an alternative as they seek to lower their production costs and increase rates of labour exploitation. These peripheries have also played an important role through the downward pressure they exert on the wages in developed countries, which make higher levels of competitivity and rates of profit possible. In effect,

> the former 'socialist' countries are integrated into the global cheap-labor economy. Despite idle factories and high levels of unemployment in the former German Democratic Republic, it was more profitable for German capitalism to expand its manufacturing base in Eastern Europe.[2]

More generally (including the insertion of southeast Asia, eastern Europe, as well as China and Russia),[3] one could illustrate how the presumption that living labour is the sole source of value and surplus value underscored the incorporation of these new territories into capital valorisation and accumulation, which resulted in a significant increase both to the mass and rate of surplus value.

If we consider the world of work as a system of social relations, the process of exploitation intrinsic to capital accumulation and centralisation on a planetary scale should be clearly in view. Under the logic of parasitic capitalism, this process has been faced with increasing challenges to the production of value and surplus value, which in turn has lead the business sector, the general agent of capital, to compensate for its losses by resorting to greater

---

2 Chossudovsky, *Globalization*, 75.
3 Giovanni Alves, "Crise de valorização e desmedida do capital. Breve ensaio sobre a natureza da crise estrutural do capital," in *Capital trabajo y nueva organización obrera*, edited by Esthela Gutiérrez, Dídimo Castillo and Adrián Sotelo, 15–39 (Ciudad de México: Siglo XXI Editores, 2011).

rates of exploitation wherever the economic, political, juridical and institutional conditions will allow, or where they can be created. We see this particularly in sectors specializing in the production of natural resources and foodstuffs, and in the exportation of cheap labour from the dependent regions to imperialist developed countries like the United States and the European Union (a territory with an area of more than 4.3 million square kilometres and 500 million habitants); even in advanced capitalist countries and their *new peripheries,* which formed as the product of the international division of labour and the expansion of the range of productive activities by transnational capital, bringing the latter into the sphere of capitalist accumulation of the hegemonic countries of the European Union. Thus, "[t]hanks to its expansion into Eastern and Central Europe, the EU boasts a larger GDP than that of the US."[4] This new configuration of the European Union,

> ...represents an authentic structural change that has incorporated a true labour periphery into the single market, both in terms of wages and working conditions. This has facilitated the process of reducing, not only working conditions, but the participation of workers in the value added by their labour throughout the territory of the European Union; in particular in the countries with greater social gains, independently of whether labour policies continue to be managed at the level of the states, and even more so under these circumstances.[5]

The disintegration of the socialist bloc provided the foundation for the construction of *new peripheries,* particularly in the sphere of the European Union and its hegemonic powers (basically Germany, France, England, Italy and Spain, the latter two representing 30 percent of the GDP of the eurozone). From the perspective of the world of work and its multiple relations and contradictions, this made it possible to introduce elements associated with labour super-exploitation which then became part of a regime aimed at restoring the conditions of capital valorisation and profitability. The new peripheries would go on to play such a role, and moreso in the current context of recession in the European Union.

In this way, capital resolved a spatial-temporal challenge inflicted by the overproduction and capitalist crises of the 1980s. The disintegration of the Soviet Union and the socialist bloc following the imposition of the Washington Consensus served the hegemonic countries of the European

---

4   Alex Callinicos, *Imperialism and Global Political Economy* (Cambridge: Polity Press, 2009), 214.
5   Arriola & Vasapollo, *Flexibles,* 178.

Union perfectly, providing opportunities to develop their production processes, access to a skilled and cheap workforce, and to the prevailing wage differential within former socialist countries (see Table 9). As a result, big European capital managed to displace the role played by older underdeveloped economies, in particular, those of Latin America, in relative terms:

> The role played at the beginning of the 20th century by underdeveloped regions of Africa, Asia or Latin America would be occupied by the 'formerly socialist countries' by the end of the same century. Instead of making incursions in agrarian and primitive regions, contemporary capitalism has found vast markets of consumers, with a trained workforce for manufacturing complex products. But as occurred in the past, these geographical displacements have not eliminated the original tensions. The contradictions which capital transfers to the periphery tend to take their toll later on the centre itself.[6]

If it is true that the newly-balkanised regions of really-existing socialism have become functional for capitalist firms in the centre, they have certainly not displaced the underdeveloped territories of the older peripheries, as this author suggests. To our mind, the role of the older peripheries has been reconceived for a new, more complex and contradictory international division of labour currently being consolidated in keeping with the needs of a multipolar regime where, in addition to the traditional imperialism of the United States and the European Union, new regional powers with hegemonic pretentions (in the case of China, India and Pakistan, for example) have emerged.

The *new peripheries* (distinct from the *old peripheries,* particularly those that emerged in Latin America during historical processes of decolonisation of the first three decades of the 19th century) were formalised with the Treaty of Lisbon and resulted in the establishment of a distinct socio-economic structure containing at least three 'Europes' operating as distinct centres and (new) peripheries:

1. The 'eurozone' with the 17 states that have adopted the euro (Austria, Belgium, Cyprus, Estonia, Germany, Finland, France, Greece, Ireland, Italy, Luxembourg, Malta, the Netherlands, Portugal, Slovakia, Slovenia and Spain).

---

6   Claudio Katz, "Los cambios en la rivalidad interimperial," *Rebelión*, 24 July 2011, accessed 19 December 2014, http://www.rebelion.org/noticia.php?id=132805.

2. The rich countries situated at the margin of the Euro: Britain, Denmark and Switzerland.
3. The peripheries: one on the southern flank of the Union on the Mediterranean, managed by France; the other the eastern part of the union managed by Germany.[7]

These new peripheries now fulfil a series of functions assigned by both the international division of labour and by regional political and geo-economic dynamics which, in this case, are limited to the European context and to multinational firms based in core countries like Germany and France who have relocated to relatively less developed areas such as Hungary, the Czech Republic, Romania and Poland where real wages are much lower, there is little union organisation and activism, and where working conditions are deteriorating.

These countries operate as platforms for receiving capital and companies that have decided to relocate to make the most of competitive advantages in terms of geographic location, wage differentials, flexible workweeks, lax or absent labour laws, weak union activism and low rates of unionisation, as well as the limited capacity for collective bargaining to defend their gains, the rights of workers and to increase real salaries, as well as the disposition of neoliberal governments to tolerate transnational corporations. They exert pressure on companies from developed countries, whose respective bourgeoisies and governments in turn blackmail their working classes and the world of work (for example, with the threat of offshoring or the closure of companies as in the case of the Germans) so as to lower wage costs, thereby increasing the rate of exploitation and accentuating competition between workers for precarious job posts in a context of limited job opportunities and few or no social provisions, such as unemployment insurance and pensions.

With the presumption that super-exploitation can be deployed at any moment in the countries of advanced capitalism (through wage cuts, increasing the intensity or length of the working day), the new peripheries compete with older ones (like Latin America) to attract and retain foreign investments, firms and technology drawn by a cheap workforce. For their part, imperialist countries take advantage of the situation to deepen social inequality, all to benefit rates of profitability and the expansion of their business activities. Thus, if the older peripheries previously

---

7 Ramón Fernández Durán, "Profundización de la Europa del capital," *Rebelión*, 22 July 2011, accessed 19 December 2014, http://www.rebelion.org/noticia.php?id=110089.[Originally published in *Revista Pueblos 42* (June 2010)].

served as platforms for the expansion of international capital, today the new peripheries fulfil this role at a regional level, while exerting pressure on the original ones so that they are forced to deepen neoliberal policies and to adjust their economies to the logic of trade and the easy profits of big international monopoly capital.

In this context, structural adjustment and stabilisation policies of international organisations have taken on a new role with respect to underdeveloped countries; for example, by displacing investments towards these regions and simultaneously pressuring the old peripheries to attract investments following macroeconomic adjustments and the imposition of social austerity. Sooner or later neoliberal policies introduced by big capital in Greece, Spain, Ireland, Portugal, Italy and England (and by extension, the European Union as a whole) will impact the Latin American peripheries dependent on its growth rates, to the detriment of wages and social spending.

All of these functions (investment platforms, worsening work conditions and labour markets, competition between old and new peripheries, and the deepening of neoliberal policies) lead capital to invest its resources in the new peripheries (outsourcing) and to redefine its role within the international division of labour to the detriment of the industrial, service and, rather explosively, agricultural sectors of underdeveloped countries. Needless to say, this scenario has had massive implications for the populations in question, above all its inflationary impact on general food consumption.

In the European Union, the effect of this 'labour periphery' has been to reduce wages, increase exploitation of and competition between workers and, ultimately, to introduce super-exploitation (or at least some of its modalities).[8] This periphery, then, has taken on that historical, congenital role of the dependent social formation, operating with its own *peculiar and constituent mechanisms*. But today, in the era of capitalist globalisation, with the extension of the labour law of value and prices of production on a global scale, it has been projected onto the international economy *operationally* with the standardisation of technological processes, with economic crisis, flexible automation, technological innovations, labour flexibility and the recurrent financial and real estate crisis throughout the system;[9] all this made possible by the globalisation of the

---

8   Recall that super-exploitation generally combines modalities, but in such a way that the remuneration of the worker falls below the value of his or her labour power. If this latter condition is not met, super-exploitation cannot be proven to exist.

9   Sotelo, *A reestruturação*, 59.

law of value, its planetary extension, and simultaneously, because the regime of super-exploitation has begun to be implemented gradually in the developed countries of the core as a mechanism to counteract the structural crisis, the financial deficit of the State and recurring problems with the profit margins of big business. This new geostrategic and geopolitical configuration of the 'new Europe' of transnational and imperialist capital is plotting a new map of the new international division of labour, of new and old peripheries, which will impact international relations, trade, national competitivity and economic, social and political processes the world over.[10]

The Character of Super-exploitation under Advanced Capitalism

For Marini, the global system has been constituted, first, according to the needs of the capitalist economies of advanced industrialised countries, which are themselves based on relative surplus value extracted by means of increasing labour productivity and, second, by dependent and underdeveloped economies and societies based on greater rates of exploitation of the workforce where the productive apparatus is separated from the consumption needs of mass workers (see Chapter 4). So situated, the author sets out two historical processes of dependent development in Latin America. The first process, following the colonial economy which was also capitalist in nature,[11] involved the existence of an economy centred primarily on exports whose problems of realisation, overproduction and contradictory processes of capital accumulation were subordinated to the dynamic and performance of the rate of profit of imperialist countries. The second process concerns the development of a national economy (which nonetheless continued to export primary materials and foodstuffs) based on import substitution industrialisation for the domestic market. This, to quote Marini, allows the laws of development to manifest fully, "which always represents a particular expression of the general laws governing the system as a whole."[12]

The point here is that issues associated with the circulation and realisation of capital (which emerge and are sharpened with the effects of labour super-exploitation) no longer correspond entirely to the international economy as

---

10   On this theme, see Jalife-Rahme, *El híbridomundo*.

11   Sergio Bagú, *Economía de la sociedad colonial. Ensayo de historia comparada de América Latina* (Mexico: Editorial Grijalbo, Consejo Nacional para la Cultura y las Artes, 1992).

12   Marini, *Dialéctica*, 85.

they did under the auspices of the export economy but, rather, derive from their *own national and dependent economic cycle*. This factor renders the internal sphere of production from that of circulation, and those sectors of production and consumption of commodities destined for internal markets and driven by middle and upper class demand are developed on a broad scale. Such sectors, whose expansion developed in conjunction with import-substitution industrialisation historically, enjoy a concentration of national and foreign investment, the markets for skilled workers, and enclaves controlled by large transnational corporations.

This second process took place, broadly speaking, from the Second World War to the beginning of the eighties. But starting in the mid-1960s, the expansion of sumptuary industries in the dependent economy would be marked by structural limitations to their processes of realisation due to income concentration (spurred by the super-exploitation of labour and other mutations, such as labour precariousness and unemployment), as well as to the strong dependency on importations, above all the means of production, technology and scientific knowledge. Amongst other measures, the intervention of the State in the dependent economy became strategic and central to the effort to counteract these grave problems and to stimulate capitalist development in the region by subsidizing (both internal and external) demand, securing areas of investment abroad through the operations of state-owned enterprises, proffering intergovernmental credit and guaranteeing the private operations of certain major companies from countries like Mexico and Brazil (the so-called 'translatinas') in other countries of Latin America or the African continent. As Marini suggested,

> The extreme concentration of income governing the region was the necessary counterpart of the stratification seen at the level of the productive apparatus. Moreover, this made the direct intervention of the State, which not only acted to create demand but also to overcome obstacles to the realisation of production and even encouraged it artificially, absorbing part of the costs, indispensible.[13]

However, rather than attempting to resolve challenges to realisation by extending the domestic market and incorporating the consumption of workers (as took place historically in the classical economies), capital and the State in the

---

13   Ruy Mauro Marini, "La acumulación capitalista mundial y el subimperialismo," *Cuadernos Políticos* 12 (April-June 1977): 32.

dependent economies opted to utilise other mechanisms in keeping with the prevailing pattern of accumulation and reproduction of the period. First, the importation of technology and foreign capital destined for investment in the industrial sector (to the obvious detriment of agriculture) aimed to elevate the productive capacity of labour and to counteract realisation problems of commodities. This explains the great interest of foreign capital in spurring the process of industrialisation of the dependent economy through the establishment of its transnational companies, a phenomenon which Marini characterises as the extension of imperialist integration of the productive systems following the Second World War.[14] And second, foreign capital and the extensive use of imported technology stimulated super-exploitation and the increase of unemployment which, in turn, resulted in the generation of new problems of realisation. To this end, State intervention and inflationary policies were extended in order to transfer the purchasing power of the popular classes (forcefully impoverished following the reduction of real wages and the unanticipated increase of the reserve army of labour) to the rich; those already benefiting from the system and in possession of a purchasing power sufficient enough to drive the productive sectors and industries needed to meet market demand for luxury consumption.

Finally, the above resources, having been exhausted (the result of the contradictions of dependent capitalism and, in particular, its own capitalist cycle and the dynamic of labour super-exploitation), the solution sought once again at the end of the seventies would be the global market, in a kind of parody of the old export economy; except that this time its bases would be modern industry, agriculture and mineral extraction. This strategy negated the need to correct internal structural imbalances (something proposed, for example, by neostructuralism) by incorporating popular consumption into the domestic market which, in turn, would have clearly required a general strategy to increase the purchasing power of workers that would begin, at the very least, with wage increments to equal the value of their labour.

Such a situation is currently completely unthinkable in countries like Mexico, where real average wages have been plummeting since the mid-seventies. This stage corresponds to the development of neoliberalism both globally and very intensely in Latin America more than three decades ago although, as Perry Anderson points out, its historical origin dates back to the post-World War II period in Europe and the United States where they emerged as a reaction against the 'interventionist and welfare state.' The framing of this critique was provided by

---

14   See his book, *Subdesarrollo y revolución – 5ª edición* (Mexico: Siglo XXI Editores, 1974).

the Austrian Friedrich von Hayek, whose 1944 book *The Road to Serfdom* would go on to earn him the Nobel Prize in 1974.[15] In a text that Marini considered a complement to his *Dialéctica de la dependencia*, he summarises this in the following way:

> ...we could say that the cycle of capital in the dependent economy is characterized by a series of particularities. Amongst them, the role played by foreign capital in the first phase of circulation, both in the form of money and of the commodity, as well as in the fact that production determines transfers of surplus value (which will become visible in the second phase of circulation), fixes extraordinary surplus value and develops it on the basis of the superexploitation of labour. Both facts lead quickly to the concentration of capital and to monopolisation, while the structure of production becomes divorced from the consumption needs of the masses. The distortion in income distribution originating from this dynamic in the second phase of circulation energizes the sector best able to sustain the development of industries producing sumptuary goods, compounding this distortion to the extent that such industries expand their production and demand more market space. The limits against which this second phase of circulation hits, both in the transfer of surplus value abroad and by the deformation of the internal income structure, lead it to search for the realisation of part of its commodities on the world market, with which the circle of dependency of the capitalist cycle comes to a close abroad....[16]

The profound changes that took place during the 1970s, both economically as well as politically and socially, unleashed a true transition towards a new capitalist global order. In Latin America, this transition manifested in the recreation of its countries into authentic export platforms, based on patterns of capitalist accumulation and reproduction specialising in the production of one or two products destined for international markets, a process that would go on to determine the new profile of societies and the world of labour under neoliberal policies.

---

15   Perry Anderson, "Balance del neoliberalismo." In *Pos-neoliberalismo. As políticas sociais e o estado democrático*, edited by Emir Sader and Pablo Gentili, 9–23 (São Paulo: Paz e Terra, 1995).

16   Ruy Mauro Marini, "El ciclo del capital en la economía dependiente" in *Mercado y dependencia*, edited by Úrsula Oswald (Mexico: Nueva Imagen, 1979), 55.

The Hegemony of Relative Surplus Value in Capitalism and Labour Super-exploitation

One of the common threads in dependency theory lies in determining the relation between relative surplus value (defined earlier) and the super-exploitation of labour since, "The problem is in *determining the character that the production of relative surplus value and increasing labour productivity assumes in the dependent economy.*"[17] As such, it is crucial to consider two key issues: First, why is it so difficult for relative surplus value in the dependent economy to take root, to become the hegemonic basis of the system of production and labour, as occurred in the countries of classical capitalism? And second, why is it that, particularly when the strategy of import substitution industrialisation developed in Latin America, labour super-exploitation continues to subsume relative surplus value, hindering it from becoming hegemonic? For us, the centre of the process of dependency and labour super-exploitation stems from this problematic. In this context, the latter issue cannot be reduced and defined simply as a 'violation' of the value of labour power, as some authors maintain. We consider that what prevailed historically in and what is currently *specific to and characteristic* of dependent economies is a mode of dependent production (to be sure, articulated with the global capitalist system) built upon a system of super-exploitation that takes on certain specificities, and which systematically hinders the extension of relative surplus value to the heart of the process of capitalist accumulation and reproduction.

In relation to the super-exploitation of labour, Marini shows that,

> ...the three mechanisms so identified (the intensification of labour, the extension of the working day, and the expropriation of part of the labour necessary for the worker to replace his or her labour power) give shape to a mode of production based exclusively on the greater exploitation of the worker, and not on the development of his or her productive capacity. This is consistent with the low level of development of the productive forces in the Latin American economy, but also with the kinds of activities carried out there. In effect, more than in manufacturing where an increase in workload implies at the very least a greater expenditure of raw materials, in the extractive industries and in agriculture, the effect of increasing labour on the elements of constant capital are much less evident; it being possible, through the simple action of man over nature, to

---

17   Marini, *Dialéctica*, 100 (italics in the original).

increase the wealth produced without any additional capital. It is understood that, in these circumstances, productive activity is based primarily on the extensive and intensive use of labour power: this allows reducing the value composition of capital which, coupled with the intensification of the rate of exploitation of labour, makes it so that the rates of surplus value and of profit are raised simultaneously.[18]

As can be inferred from this, the complexity of the dependent economy, inserted into the contradictory and uneven dynamic of the global capitalist system, undermines the notion that super-exploitation can be reduced to a simple 'violation' of the value of labour power. To do so convincingly, it would be necessary to have designed an 'ideal model' which (supposedly) also expresses the ideal value that labour power should hold. Beyond this statistical and empirical exercise, we believe that what really exists is a *mode of dependent capitalist production that is complex, multifaceted, contradictory and problematic* and which has *its own cycle of reproduction* that exacerbates the exploitation of labour power and of nature. This is mediated by multiple factors, including the dynamic provided by hegemonic capitalism, the authoritarian characteristics of the State, growing unemployment and underemployment of the workforce, inflationary and deflationary trends of the economy, contradictory dynamics of international trade, the narrowness of domestic consumer and labour markets, and the relative possibilities of regional capitalist expansion to realise production on global markets, as is now taking place under the new pattern of reproduction of dependent capitalism, specifically productive specialisation for the global market. In Latin America and other dependent regions now devoting increasing proportions of their production to external markets (today, in particular, involving massive investments in the production of biofuels and raw materials for export), agricultural resources previously for popular consumption have now been converted to satisfy the energy needs of dominant capitalism, which now includes new centres such as China, which projects itself as a regional and global power. Amongst South American economics, for example, this is particularly significant in Argentina and Brazil.

The substantial difference between advanced and dependent capitalism lies in the fact that, in the former, relative surplus value has long been hegemonic in its productive system, while in the latter, it has been subordinated to older forms of capitalist production (absolute surplus value and super-exploitation, both of which preceded relative surplus value). This is due to the fact that

---

18   Marini, ibid., 40–41.

...conditions created by the superexploitation of labour in the dependent capitalist economy tend to hinder its transition from the production of absolute surplus value to that of relative surplus value as the dominant from of relations between capital and labour. The result is the disproportionate pull that extraordinary surplus value assumes in the dependent system, which corresponds to the expansion of the industrial reserve army and the relative stranglehold of the realisation capacity of production. More than mere accidents in the context of dependent development or elements of a transitional order, these phenomena are manifestations of the particular way in which the general law of accumulation affects the dependent economy. Ultimately, it is once again to the superexploitation of labour that we must refer in order to analyse them.[19]

From the beginning, advanced capitalism articulated with and subordinated absolute surplus value (the extension of the working week and intensification of the labour process) to relative surplus value, at least since the great period of the industrial revolution in England, and gradually incorporated workers into the consumption of goods produced by the factories of big industry. It was this that pushed Marx, in Chapter XIV of *Capital–Volume III*, to perceive the empirical possibility of labour super-exploitation (the reduction of wages below the value of labour power)[20] but, more so as a product of competition and the conjuncture, one geared more towards counteracting the tendency of the rate of profit to fall, than as a structural tendency and a regular, secular feature in the general analysis of capital. But this was largely congruent with the methodological premise maintained throughout *Capital* that, as we saw earlier, presupposes that the value of labour power (like that of any other commodity) always corresponds to its market price.[21] Later on, in a period characterised by the sociology of work associated with Taylorist/Fordist systems of mass production, workers recently incorporated to the assembly line were deemed to matter both as producers of the commodities produced by big industry (for example, automobiles) as their consumers.[22]

The merit and novelty of Marini's proposal regarding dependency theory is that he positioned the category of super-exploitation (which was left out of the general analysis of capital by Marx for the reasons discussed earlier) as the core and

---

19   Marini, ibid., 100.

20   Marx, *Capital – Volume III*, 235.

21   See note 9 of chapter 4.

22   In this respect, see the magnificent work by Braverman, *Labor*.

guiding principle of capitalist development in underdeveloped socio-economic formations at the periphery of the global system, allowing them to be differentiated historically and structurally from the development of classical capitalism.[23]

Applying the category to contemporary capitalism, Marini identifies three conditions previously addressed by capital towards the end of the eighties to usher in a new stage of history; a shift signalled by the fall of the Berlin Wall in 1989, the disintegration of the Soviet Union, and the imperialist invasion of Iraq by the United States in 1991, in addition to by the large scale application of computing technology to material and immaterial production and to telecommunications, or the third industrial revolution. First, the degree of labour exploitation was heightened throughout the system in order to increase the mass of surplus value which, he adds, was only possible following the defeat of labour and popular movements in the capitalist centre, as well as those of the periphery, including Latin America. Second, the concentration of capital was intensified in advanced economies to secure investments for research and development and modern industry requiring strong transfers of value from the dependent countries of Latin America (so-called *unequal exchange*) and which, in turn, increased capital accumulation. As a result, issues of employment, wages, marginality and social immiseration were aggravated for broad sectors of the population. The third condition involved expanding the scale of the market to facilitate the considerable investments that would be required to modernise the industrial apparatus.

All of these processes, Marini concludes, reinvigorated the central laws and mechanisms of the system, "...particularly the law of value...which operates through the comparison of the real value of goods (in other words, of the labour time invested in their creation), understood as the time required by inputs and means of production, as well as the reproduction of the labour power."[24] In the 1990s, these three conditions facilitated the conversion of the Latin American

---

23 Here, it is worth noting the observation by Vania Bambirra, ignored by most critics of dependency theory, that in the strictest sense there is no "dependency theory" of the capitalist mode of production as such, "...because this was already set out by Marx; nor of the 'dependent capitalist mode of production' per se, because this does not exist; it is rather the study of dependent capitalist socio-economic formations...that is capable of capturing the specific combination of the modes of production which have coexisted in Latin America under the hegemony of capitalism." Bambirra, *Teoría*, 26.

24 Ruy Mauro Marini, "Preface," in *México, dependencia y modernización*, written by Adrián Sotelo Valencia (Mexico: El Caballito, 1990), 9–12.

economy into a neoliberal dependent economy based upon a pattern of accumulation and capital reproduction subordinated to the capitalist dynamic of the hegemonic countries of advanced capitalism and increasingly, to the reproductive cycle of the Chinese economy. The structural configuration of the Latin American economy turned towards the global market, and based upon reproduction patterns centred around processes of 'reprimarisation' and technology imports from central countries, is an accurate reflection of a new form of dependency that has made the region more vulnerable to the external contradictions that global capitalist accumulation has entailed in the 21st century.

Critiques and Counter-critiques

The debate over the extent to which super-exploitation has been extended to the advanced countries is currently embryonic, and restricted to certain theoretical and fewer empirical expressions amongst a limited number of authors who have perceived the phenomenon in the context of issues associated with contemporary capitalism.[25] This is explained, in part, by recent manifestations of the phenomenon that have been extended gradually through a series of economic measures and public policies in the imperialist countries. Independently of the diverse interpretations available, there are also now themes that have allowed us to understand the phenomenon in the context of the crisis of capitalism, expressed socially and in the experience of work by a series of measures which have negatively affected wages, working time, and social consumption in countries of the European Union, the United States and others such as Japan; countries which have seen the quality of living and working conditions reduced over the last few years and where, to all appearances, there is no way out for capital, which thus continues to deepen and buttress the regime of super-exploitation in such societies.

Jaime Osorio discusses the question of labour super-exploitation in a book that turns on two central issues: the theory of 'redoubled exploitation' or labour super-exploitation, in Chapter 5 and the addendum, and the theme of revolution, whereby Latin America is regarded as the weakest link in the global

---

25   In his book *Globalização, dependência e neoliberalismo na América Latina* (Rio de Janeiro: Boitempo Editorial, 2011), Carlos Eduardo Martins writes at the juncture of dependency theory, world-systems analysis and the Kondratiev cycle (which the author considers to have originated an expansive phase of capitalism from 1994 to today), and analyses the potential extension of super-exploitation to the system as a whole (see in particular chapter 6 which is dedicated to this issue).

imperialist system that has nonetheless internalised the contradictions of the latter.[26] Here we will address the first point. The author discusses the plausibility of the introduction of labour super-exploitation to advanced capitalism, and the issue of its generalisation throughout the system as a whole. He asserts that,

> what defines the essence of dependent capitalism is redoubled exploitation, or the superexploitation of the workforce, a term which attends to the mechanism through which the *value* of this force is systematically *violated*.[27]

Consequently, in contrast to advanced capitalism "in dependent economies, this form of exploitation is located at the centre of capitalist accumulation."[28] In his addendum, Osorio insists on this point when he argues that

> With this concept of superexploitation, an attempt is made to account for a form of labour exploitation in which the value of labour power is violated on a structural, recurring basis.[29]

This 'violation,' according to the author, takes three forms: the reduction of wages below their value, the extension of the working day, and the intensification of labour.[30] The three create a structure in which "one or the other of these cases" dominates.[31] And which *dominates* in a dependent economy, he asks? The answer involves the violation of the value of labour power through the reduction of the worker's consumption fund, which is converted into a fund of accumulation by the capitalist.[32] For Osorio, exploitation can increase the productive capacity of core countries, while in dependent ones, the main forms of exploitation remain based on the violation of the value of labour power. While this method predominates in the dependent world, things occur in a distinctive way in advanced countries, according to the author, where the

---

26   Jaime Osorio, *Explotación redoblada y actualidad de la revolución. Refundación societal, rearticulación popular y nuevo autoritarismo* (Mexico: Itaca, Universidad Autónoma Metropolitana-Unidad Xochimilco, 2009).

27   Ibid., 109 (italics in the original).

28   Ibid., 128.

29   Ibid., 125 (italics in the original).

30   Ibid., 113–14.

31   Ibid., 115.

32   Ibid., 139.

intensification of labour and the extension of working time are more prevalent;[33] we can see the latter in measures to increase the working day in the
European Union,[34] while wages (and consequently, the consumption fund of
workers) have been reduced.

> In the central or imperialist economies, the intensification of labour and
> the extension of the working day are the dominant forms of labour super-
> exploitation, the payment of salaries below the value of labour power
> having less weight there.[35]

But this statement is contradicted when the author affirms that, in the advanced
countries, longer hours of work and labour intensity may also exhaust workers
prematurely; while these hours may be paid, they nonetheless fail to replenish
the years snatched from the workers, so that ultimately, "the total value of
labour power has been violated."[36] If this indeed takes place, we would ask
what then happens to the specificity of dependent capitalism, in which setting
the *total* value of labour power is also violated? As we have seen, the characteristic that supposedly sets each formation apart vanishes, and labour super-
exploitation (identified simply with the violation of the value of labour power)
also loses its specificity, although the author attempts to correct this ambi-
guity by stating that, "Both kinds of capitalism are superexploiters of labour,
although in distinct ways."[37] However, even if they are "superexploiters" in "distinct ways," dependency still disappears as a historical-structural category that
is distinct from advanced capitalism under this logic. So are only the forms
(rather than the *essence*) of labour super-exploitation distinct in each 'kind' of
capitalism? It would be beneficial to reflect further on this point, particularly
in light of the political and ideological consequences implied for the social
struggles of workers.

   A phenomenon as complex as super-exploitation cannot be reduced to
the simple violation of the value of labour power (and neither can the work
and thought of Marini be interpreted in such a way) since a number of

---

33   Ibid., 134.
34   Ibid., 118. This speaks to the adoption of a directive issued by the Council of Employment
      and Social Policy Ministers of the 27 member countries of the European Union in 2008, by
      which the 48-hour workweek (established in 1917 by the ILO) was repealed. Now, the
      employer and employee must agree to greater working time, even up to 65 hours of aver-
      age work weekly.
35   Ibid., 141.
36   Ibid.
37   Ibid.

structural and super-structural factors would thus be abstracted from the analysis, including the degree of industrialisation, capitalist cycles of the dependent economy,[38] social and political struggles, public policies, and the relative strength or weakness of unions and working class organisations. Nonetheless, if this were the case, it would be enough to simply 'respect' the value of labour power (for example, as the progressive governments that have emerged in Latin America over the last few years have instituted) in order to 'eliminate' super-exploitation as a foundation and axis of dependency.

Brazilian wage policy provides a window to this discussion of how to assess the relation between wages and the value of labour power. On the cusp of the structural, real estate and financial crisis of global capitalism starting in 2007–08, the Lula government based its programme for economic growth on the internal market, in the best neo-developmentalist tradition, and on a policy of raising real wages in the country (in particular, in the manufacturing sector for production line workers). Could such policies overcome dependency, by adjusting real wages in order to bring them 'closer' to the value of labour power and, thus, 'put an end to the violation' of said value by bringing them into alignment (as the government officially proposed) with the prevailing wages in countries like the United States?[39] At the end of 2009, the Brazilian state redefined its wage policy by establishing a 'commitment' to recover the wages levels prevalent in 1996 (when they supposedly most approximated those of the United States) by adjusting wages against the equivalent salaries of the major economies globally. Beginning in 2010, a plan to increase the minimum wage annually was issued and called the 'minimum wage valorisation policy'.[40] This policy set out an average increase of 5.87 percent above inflation and represented a nominal increase of 9.68 percent.

Even more importantly, in 2010 the Brazilian government sent a bill to Congress with three proposals to readjust the minimum wage, which

---

38   "The deep contradiction that characterized the cycle of capital in this economy and its effects on labour exploitation will have a decisive impact on the course that the Latin American industrial economy takes, explaining many of the problems and the tendencies at present." Marini, *Dialéctica*, 54–55.

39   On this point, see Alianza Global Jus Semper, "Gráficas de Brecha Salarial Manufacturera para Brasil frente a economías desarrolladas y 'emergentes' seleccionadas, con datos salariales y PPC disponibles (1996–2009)," accessed 2 February 2015, http://www.jussemper .org/Inicio/Recursos/Recursos%20Laborales/GBS/Resources/GrafsbrechasBras2006.pdf.

40   Provisional Measure 474 of 23 December 2009 provides for the minimum wages from 1 January 2010, which provided guidelines for the promotion of a policy for increasing the minimum wage from 2011 to 2023, cited in Alianza Global Jus Semper, "Gráficas", 17.

provided guidelines for the periods of 2012–2015, 2016–2019, and 2020–2023. The plan demonstrated a clear intention to gradually close the wage gap with wages of the major economies by 2023. The specific formula used by Brazil (which would come into effect in 2011) is the sum of the national consumer-price index plus rate of GDP growth, if it is positive. For example, if inflation is 5 percent in a single year and GDP grows by 4 percent, the nominal increase will be 9 percent and the real 4 percent.[41]

If we were to assume with an altruistic panglossian candour that one day this positive outcome will in fact materialise (something which the government, now under the administration of Dilma Rousseff, supposes will take place by 2023), will it put an end to dependency in Brazil, as some authors have wrongly maintained with regard to a country that now ranks amongst the 'great' powers of the world, including the select group of BRICS? In this regard, the conclusion of a recent historical-structural analysis of recent Brazilian economy by Antunes is instructive:

> With this double character (being the producer of durable consumer goods for the domestic market and of primary products and manufactures for the global market), Brazilian capitalism has become the eighth largest economy in the world, despite always maintaining a dependent structure that is subordinated to imperialism...a kind of *monopoly capitalism of the dependent and subordinated State.*[42]

It is no secret that, since the 1970s under the military dictatorship, speculation has abounded surrounding the emergence of Brazil as a 'regional power', thus having ostensibly bypassed its status as a dependent country. Former President Cardoso has come to dismiss the existence of 'dependency,' opting instead to speak of a beneficial 'interdependence', which holds the possibility of transforming the country into a 'developed' one. However, the status of developed country in the international division of labour has never been reached, nor has it by other countries in the dependent sphere and Brazil's *subimperialist* character as initially diagnosed by Marini has only been reaffirmed. In this regard, referring to the position maintained by Brazil in the international economy of the 1970s, in which it preferred to 'unlock capitalist accumulation' through the development of its nuclear and defence industries, Marini made three inferences:

---

41   Ibid.

42   Antunes, *O continente do labor*, 136–37 (italics in the original).

First, the claim that the global capitalist crisis, the last resort of which lies in confrontations between the major capitalist powers, has not only precipitated the Brazilian economic crisis, but has also given Brazil the possibility of overcoming it. In effect, both with regard to nuclear energy and its relation to the defence industry, today the Brazilian state utilises the fierce competition between the United States and Western Europe (particularly Germany), as well as Japan, to secure resources provided by the global circulation of capital, means of production and technology. *Brazil will not overcome dependency by these means*; rather, by diversifying the means by which it articulates with global capitalism, space will open for it to pursue its project of industrial development and, on this basis, its claim as a middling power in the global scheme of power distribution. In other words, the Brazilian state is utilizing inter-imperialist contradictions to guarantee the realization of its own sub-imperialist project.[43]

One must clearly also consider the emergence of China as a competitive protagonist on the international stage beside and against traditional imperialist countries like the United States, Japan and the European Union; and, within the latter, countries such as Germany and France against England, in relation to strategies of political integration and the structural crisis that has shaken the region and the Eurozone. On the other hand, it may also be said that Argentina in recent years (following the crisis of 2001–2002) has experienced unprecedented growth (around 7.5 percent on average between 2003 and 2010) sustained by primary exports but in a manner that has in no way overcome dependency, as suggested in a recent analysis by Julio Gambina:

> Argentina remains a country dependent on global capitalism, subordinated to the power of transnational corporations; for this reason, foreign capital dominates strategic sectors of the local economy, be it in agriculture, industry or services. The presence of Argentinean companies amongst the transnationals of the region, the *translatinas*, does not alter this marked character; to the contrary, it confirms that capital can only function effective it if reaches the height of global competition.[44]

This illustrates the continuing validity of the dependency thesis, and its vital resource, labour super-exploitation, even in economies that have maintained

---

43   Marini, "Estado," 82.
44   Julio C. Gambina, "Economía a fines del 2011," *Rebelión*, 20 December 2011, accessed 21 January 2015, http://www.rebelion.org/noticia.php?id=141613.

higher rates of growth when compared to industrialised countries, and where variables such as the global market are essential to such performance.

The discussion can in no way be predicated on reducing super-exploitation to the simple violation of the value of labour power in economies as complex as those of Latin America. Rather, given the historical presence and structural creation of a *regime* of super-exploitation that generated its own economic cycle, dependent to different degrees and in different ways on the international economy and the large economic, productive and hegemonic centres of advanced capitalism, what we can say is that an *average* remuneration of the workforce was established, based upon the dominance of the three forms that super-exploitation takes (generally combined in practice) when workers are not fully paid: a) the extension of the working day; b) the intensification of labour, and c) the reduced consumption of the worker beyond its normal limit.

In this respect, two observations can be made. In order to be able to speak of super-exploitation at all, be it under the auspices of an extended working day or of increased intensity in the labour process, part of that surplus labour (be it extensive or intensive) must cease to be rewarded to the worker; if not, there is no super-exploitation, even though the worker suffers increased fatigue that reduces her or his useful life as a worker, and rather, she or he remains subject to the 'normal' mechanisms of exploitation. Thus, Marini refers to super-exploitation as a system that combines three modalities:

> The three mechanisms identified (the intensification of labour, the extension of the working day, and the expropriation of part of the labour necessary for the worker to replace his or her labour power) give shape to a mode of production founded exclusively on the greater exploitation of the worker, and not on the development of his or her productive capacity. This is congruent with the low level of development of the productive forces in the Latin American economy, but also with the kinds of activities which are realized there. In capitalist terms, these mechanisms (which can also occur, and normally do, in combination) mean that work is remunerated below its value; thus, they correspond to a superexploitation of labour.[45]

As we can see, for Marini the *combination* of forms of super-exploitation leads consistently to a situation wherein labour is paid below its value. Turning to the particular issue of labour intensity, Marini suggests that, unlike productivity at the level of particular industries,

---

45   Marini, *Dialéctica*, 40–42.

[t]he increased *intensity* gives rise to a different situation, in which the individual capitalist alters neither the value nor the use value of the commodities; instead, it is expressed in the production of a greater mass of commodities whose unit value does not change, resulting in a mass of value and, therefore, surplus value. There is, however, no reason for the rate of surplus value to be altered once the *greater rate of intensity leads to a rise in value of labour power, with which its cost and wage must also rise. Thus, for the rate of surplus value to rise or at least for it to rise more proportionately with the increase to labour intensity, it will be necessary* (regardless of whether the price and wage of the workforce increases) *for it be remunerated below its value*; that is, to be subject to superexploitation.[46]

From the point of view of the law of labour-value, if the worker performs supplemental work, either extensively or intensively, beyond the legal limit of the working day and is paid accordingly, then super-exploitation has not taken place. Thus, it is fair to say that in any given society, there are categories of workers receiving high salaries, with high levels of professional qualification, full-time jobs complete with vested rights who are not super-exploited by capital, both in dependent countries and in the imperialist advanced ones; and low-wage, precarious workers without labour rights, who are contracted and dismissed freely by their bosses, and where the latter is reinforced by the labour reforms taking place throughout the world. The key is to determine whether super-exploitation has been implemented and developed under the hegemony of relative surplus value, with the structural limitations that this implies, as seems to be occurring in countries of advanced capitalism; or whether it is established at the same time that the development of relative surplus value (as we argue) is subordinated and blocked, as took place in countries that raised their industrialisation coefficients and developed domestic consumer and labour markets in Latin America under import-substitution industrialisation.

We bring this up to address an assertion by Osorio, charging us with something we have not in fact said, namely that,

...before the advance of mechanisms of labour superexploitation in the world system in recent decades, and in particular wage reductions, [Sotelo] states that superexploitation no longer constitutes a specific characteristic of dependent economies; rather, it is an attribute of every capitalist economy.[47]

---

46 Marini, "Plusvalía," 25 (italics in the original).
47 Osorio, *Explotación*, 139. The page on which this is supposedly asserted is not mentioned.

In fact, we stated that,

> [t]he aforementioned historical-social formations of the contemporary
> world economy are laying the foundations for the superexploitation of
> labour; with this, superexploitation would stop being exclusively a *regime*
> *proper* to dependent economies and *extend* its scope to the *developed*
> *countries* (something Marini correctly raised), including the United
> States itself. In this way, superexploitation is becoming the shackle that
> ties the new systems of labour organization together, such as post-Fordism,
> Toyotism and reengineering.[48]

This is a very different proposition to that attributed to us by the author, suggest-
ing that super-exploitation 'no longer constitutes' a specific characteristic of
dependent economies. In case there are any lingering doubts, we also argued that

> [i]f the superexploitation of labour operated as a mechanism particular
> to dependent social formations, it has more recently been projected into
> the international economy through the homogenization of technological
> processes, through crisis, flexible automation, technological innovations,
> labour flexibility and the recurring financial crisis of the system.[49]

When we say that super-exploitation has been *projected* into the international
economy, we in no way affirm that it no longer constitutes the defining characteristic of the dependent economy; an absurd proposition that leads nowhere
and rather introduces confusion and theoretical weakness. Rather, it means
that capital in its thirst for profit has no qualms or limits in its drive to exploit
the labour force, even by redoubling exploitation (the hyper-exploitation of
labour, one might say), in the effort to maintain its reproduction on an ever–
increasing scale. Finally, in the same work we state,

> In such a way, the superexploitation of labour, formerly exclusive to the
> dependent economies, has become a mechanism that has articulated with
> the methods of producing relative surplus value to which transnational
> companies and the State resort in the countries of central capitalism.[50]

---

48   Sotelo Valencia, Adrián. *La reestruturución del mundo del trabajo, superexplotación y nue-
      vos paradigmas de la organización del trabajo* (Mexico: Universidad Obrera de México,
      Editorial Ithaca, Escuela Nacional para Trabajadores, 2003), 46.
49   Ibid., 47.
50   Ibid., 51.

And what are the State and businesses in Europe now doing in terms of structural adjustment, social austerity, wage cuts and increases to the retirement
time of workers, as well as the privatisation of social security, education and
welfare? As suggested by another author in relation to the policies that big
capital has applied in Greece (and by extension, Europe),

> The measures adopted are not addressed to improving the living condi-
> tions of the Greek citizenship. The crux of the matter is something else—
> giving guarantees to financial and speculative capital, as well as to its
> junior partners, industrial capital, in order to continue exploiting the
> working class left and right, and in so doing, to end once and for all with
> the public sector, privatization its last possessions. In short, nothing new
> under the sun.[51]

What *is* new under the sun is the fact that the State and transnational corporations in advanced capitalist countries hold the reigns of mechanisms of super-
exploitation which *combine* the production of absolute and relative surplus
value under the aegis of the latter; in contrast to what occurred (and continues
to occur) in dependent capitalism, where relative surplus value was tightly
overdetermined (and in many instances, blocked) by super-exploitation which
served as the foundation of capital reproduction.

As we can see, Osorio charges us with a statement that we never made, at
least with the significance that he attributes. In another context, we suggested
that if capitalist globalisation can be explained by the continuing applicability
of the law of value and its extension globally, we can also hypothesise that the
regime of labour super-exploitation (which Marini confined to the dependent
economies of the capitalist periphery) has begun to spread significantly to
developed countries, even though it takes particular forms, including in the
new peripheries that arose from the disintegration of the socialist bloc starting
at the end of the eighties.[52]

The quantitative magnitude of the measure of value is insufficient to guarantee reasonable rates of surplus value and substantial increases of profit (as we
saw in Chapter 3), something apparent in the low average rates of economic

---

51   Marcos Roitman Rosenmann, "¡Por favour, salven a la Unión Europea y el euro!" *La
      Jornada*, 23 July 2011,accessed 22 July 2015, http://www.jornada.unam.mx/2011/07/23/
      index.php?section=opinion&article=018a2pol.
52   Adrián Sotelo Valencia, *El mundo del trabajo en tensión. Flexibilidad laboral y fractura
      social en la década de 2000* (Mexico: Plaza y Valdés Editores, Facultad de Ciencias Políticas
      y Sociales–Universidad Nacional Autónoma de México, 2007), 58, 67.

growth witnessed in the advanced economies over the past decade, in the diversion of investments from the productive sphere to banks and stock markets, as well as to the swelling of fictitious capital. This is why globalised capital and the State have tended to generalise the regime of labour super-exploitation and to resort to all kind of policies to seize and exploit the human forces and natural resources of the planet for the benefit of so many commodities designed to guarantee the expanded reproduction of the capitalist mode of production.

In this context, and in a more concrete analytical sphere, we argue that labour super-exploitation, characterised as dependent capitalism since 1850, has today been introduced in countries of the centre of the global system as a mechanism to contain the fall in rates of profitability and capital investment without altering its essential character or replacing its centrality in dependent countries. The financial crisis is only a manifestation of mutations and adjustments at the level of macroeconomics and the world of labour: the contraction of production, reduction of productive jobs and increase of structural unemployment; and the fall of the rates of profitability and average rates of economic growth that characterise contemporary capitalism, amongst other factors. Thus, super-exploitation and flexible, precarious, and polyvalent capital-labour relations (where Toyotism and flexible automation shape new forms of labour organisation and are increasingly becoming new norms of labour and contractual relations throughout the world) constitute the core of new social relations of production particular to this stage of global crisis and restructuring.[53]

In sum, we consider that while the category of super-exploitation was historically *constituent* of Latin American economies and societies, it has recently began to operate throughout the international economy, in particular advanced countries of the capitalist system and, today, in new peripheries which have become links in the globalised chains of production of value and capitalist valorisation in Europe. The substantial difference with respect to the character of super-exploitation in force in each kind of capitalism is that, in dependent countries, it is configured and functions under the aegis of productive and labour processes based on absolute surplus value, on the intensification of labour, and on the reduction of the worker's consumption fund. In advanced capitalism, to the contrary, super-exploitation is limited to the dominant cycles of capital operating regionally and internationally under the hegemony of

---

53   Adrián Sotelo Valencia, *Crisis capitalista y desmedida del valor: un enfoque desde los Grundrisse* (Mexico: Editorial Ítaca, Facultad de Ciencias Políticas y Sociales–Universidad Nacional Autónoma de México, 2010), 54.

THE NEW MORPHOLOGY OF CAPITALISM

relative surplus value; the incessant increase of labour's productive capacity, the application of science and technology to productive and labour processes, and the internal dynamics of consumer markets energised by the purchasing power of the working classes. However, in many fractions of the working classes, wage levels have been reduced, giving shape to working populations that are low-waged, poor, precarious and polyvalent, with low purchasing power, and a limited ability to acquire the basic necessities of life.

Super-exploitation, Surplus Value and Rates of Profit

As we saw in Chapter 3, capital strives to cut socially-necessary labour time as much as possible, to prolong surplus labour with an eye to increasing the rate of profit, and self-valorisation of capital through the exploitation of labour. Ultimately, there is no other method possible of meeting the goal of producing either relative or absolute surplus value independently of or in combination with the system, despite the qualifications made earlier. For this reason, increasing the general rate of exploitation becomes a central strategy of accumulation and the rate of profit for capital. While the processes for doing so will vary from country to country, region to region and from firm to firm, depending on structural conditions and the state of class struggle, the same essential objective is being pursued.

Thus, to increase the rate of exploitation and production of surplus value, capital makes use of all available methods and resources, from longer working hours (a tendency we have recently seen in Europe), increased intensity (Toyotism and flexible automation), and the phenomenal development of productive forces through the application of scientific and technological advances (a further industrial revolution) which, over the long run, replaces labour power with machinery. One strategy to achieve this objective (broadly applied in the dependent countries) is to introduce processes of super-exploitation in the context of the production of absolute and relative surplus value, including the reduction (through its expropriation) of the consumption fund of the worker, in order to convert this portion into an *additional source* of capital accumulation. The other two sources are the total pillaging of nature and accumulation by dispossession of people, communities, and nations.[54]

The concentration and centralisation of capital facilitates the survival and expansion of hegemonic corporations through the concentration of the means

---

54   David Harvey, *El nuevo imperialismo* (Madrid: Akal, 2003).

of production, of capital, and primary materials, labour power, knowledge, and scientific research and development. This has been achieved thanks to powerful inter-capitalist competition which, while not able to create value and surplus value in and of itself, facilitates the concentration of value by changing its distribution, which benefits certain capitals to the detriment of others. In a context of crisis and the contraction of average rates of growth in advanced capitalist countries (currently, European), competition has strengthened fictitious capital in the banking sector and major stock exchanges of the world, auguring speculation and all the predictable negative consequences its implies for the world of work, social conditions, and the life of workers and the population more generally.

Since the beginning of the seventies, due both to competition and technological diffusion, there has been a marked *tendency* towards the reduction of differentials in the rates of labour exploitation in the midst of a growing, upward equalisation of such rates. As Mészáros writes,

> ...we have witnessed in the last few decades, in the form of a *downward spiral* affecting labour's standard of living in the capitalistically most advanced countries, a certain *equalization in the differential rates of exploitation*.[55]

This tendency has articulated with another cited by the author: the growing authoritarianism of the capitalist State in the developed metropole, without which the regime of labour super-exploitation could hardly function. The repressive reaction of the State to the social and political insurgency of workers against programmes of austerity and the clawing back of living and working conditions in the countries of the European Union (Greece, Spain, Portugal, Ireland, Italy, England) is indicative of the aggressive reaction of power in 'democracies' of so-called 'Western civilisation' towards social movements affected by the unilateral imposition of neoliberal policies and fratricidal capitalism intended to counteract the financial deficits of the State responsible for the crisis.

We suggested earlier that, by driving the levelling of organic compositions of capital in the global economy, technological standardisation has also increased the importance of the worker as a *source of extraordinary profit*. And so labour super-exploitation has become a key factor in the effort to confront heightened competition amongst capitals on the global scale and also to counteract the growing difficulties that capital faces in the contradictory production of value and surplus value. This thesis finds support in a recent study by

---

55   Mészáros, *Beyond Capital*, 54.

ECLAC[56] which affirms that, during the eighties and nineties, economic development in Latin America and the Caribbean was characterised by (among other things) an inability to close the gap in labour productivity in relation to the developed countries of advanced capitalism. Even during the first years of the new century, the gap widened further, both in relation to OECD countries and the global average. However, it adds, this situation began to change in 2004 when average labour productivity in the Latin American region started to grow at rates similar to the global average, and above those of the OECD. Most importantly, it concludes that this upturn has had little positive impact on real salaries in the formal sector which, in most countries, grew at lower rates, something also expressed in terms of deteriorating functional income distribution and a reduction in unit labour costs.[57] In other words, a low-wage economy was consolidated over this period, mainly in underdeveloped and dependent economies that used labour super-exploitation to sustain development projects devoted to domestic markets for luxury goods (to the detriment of popular consumption), as well as to expand exports. Chossudovsky draws our attention to,

> ...a lowering of labour costs and a decline in the levels of necessary mass consumption (basic human needs) by the large majority of the population. On the other hand, the 'recomposition' of consumption is characterised by the enlargement of 'high-income consumption' through the liberalisation of trade and the dynamic influx of imported consumer durables and luxury goods for a small segment of society. This 'decomposition/recomposition' of the national economy and its insertion into the global cheap-labour economy is predicated on the compression of internal demand (and of the levels of social livelihood: poverty, low wages and an abundant supply of cheap labour are 'inputs' on the supply side. Poverty and the reduction of production costs constitute the instrumental basis (on the supply side) for reactivating production geared towards the external market.[58]

While industrialisation occurred in many dependent economies of the capitalist periphery, increasing their average rates of productivity through the

---

56   ECLAC, *Economic Survey of Latin America and the Caribbean 2010–2011: International Integration and Macroeconomic Policy Challenges amid Global Turmoil*, Santiago de Chile, United Nations, November 2011, accessed 25 January 2015, http://repositorio.cepal.org/ bitstream/11362/1075/86/2010-2011_en.pdf.

57   ECLAC, ibid., 24.

58   Chossudovsky, *Globalization*, 78–79.

incorporation (and retention) of advanced technology (as postulated by Raúl Prebisch), it did not eliminate super-exploitation or counteract the low wages characterizing the region's labour markets. From this, we can conclude that Marini is correct when he argues that to a greater or lesser extent, any increase in productivity is inextricably linked to technological improvements; however, such progress will be quasi-independent of improvements to the social conditions and real wages enjoyed by workers, and to the functional distribution of income in society. This is because the engine of development in dependent capitalism rests primarily on industries producing sumptuary items, whether in sector I (which produces capital and intermediary goods), or sector II (which produces luxury items whose demand is satisfied by the intermediate and higher sectors of social hierarchies and, when proven inadequate in terms of providing effective demand, the world market).

The modernisation and application of information technology, telematics and microelectronics in productive and labour processes, while increasing average labour productivity, have also entailed the spread of unemployment and underemployment, which have been exacerbated in dependent and underdeveloped countries, more recently alongside labour flexibility and precariousness with the consequent loss of social and contractual rights of workers. Together these factors have implied an exponential increase in the exploitation of labour through various methods, including the extension of the work day (absolute surplus value), its intensification (relative surplus value when it is generalised to the system as a whole) and the remuneration of labour power below its value (super-exploitation). Due to this series of factors, and particularly the *tendency* towards the standardisation of technology in productive processes, which unleashes a simultaneous tendency towards the equalisation of the organic compositions of capital, labour super-exploitation has begun to operate in the productive and labour structures of developed countries. From this it can be inferred that

> ...that which was a distinctive feature (even when not operational) of the dependent economy becomes generalized to the entire system, including to the advanced centres: the generalized superexploitation of labour.[59]

Exploitation in Advanced Countries

According to Shaikh, the rate of labour exploitation in the main industrialised countries increased during the 1980s through a reduction of real wages relative

---

59   Marini, "Proceso," 65.

to average productivity, particularly in England and the United States.[60] It was precisely this slowing of the growth of real wages per hour (against an increase of labour productivity, of the rate of exploitation, and the system-wide reduction of interest rates after 1982) that explains the halting of the declining rate of profit during the Reagan administration (1979–1989) in the United States and its subsequent recovery until the end of 2007.[61] The repression and intensive state attacks on unions to break their resistance also contributed to this turnaround for capital. This policy, according to Shaikh, would fuel "the boom of the latter part of the twentieth century," which he summarises as follows:

> ...the general rate of profit was pulled out of its long slump by a concerted attack on labour which caused real wages after 1982 to grow much more slowly than in the past. ...[T]he interest rate fell sharply after 1982. ... [T]he net effect of these two historically unprecedented movement was to greatly raise the rate of profit-of-enterprise. *This* is the secret of the great boom that began in the 1980s.[62]

The effort to reduce necessary labour time (nt) in order to increase surplus labour-time (st) is an historical process that has encompassed an increasing range of countries with distinctive degrees of industrial and technological development (in other words, organic compositions of capital). Figure 1[63] illustrates the increasing rate of exploitation in the United States, expressed in terms of an increase of surplus value (notably since the beginning of the 2000s), which has been strengthened by restrictive policies and rising unemployment, currently fluctuating between 9 and 12.5% of the total workforce.[64]

---

60   Shaikh, "The First."

61   Ibid. In this article, Shaikh explains that the real interest rate in the United States (but also in the majority of industrialised countries) evolved in two phases: one which saw a sharp rise from 0.59 percent in 1947 to 14.03 percent in 1981; and a second, between 1981 and 2009 which conversely experienced a several fall, from 14.03 percent to 0.16 percent respectively. As of the date of writing (December 2011), the latter levels have practically been maintained.

62   Shaikh, "TheFirst," 50, 52.

63   I thank Efrain Flores Lopez for the digitisation of the images.

64   Alfredo Jalife-Rahme, *El fin de una era. Turbulencias de la globalización* (Mexico: Orfila, 2007), 123. In an attempt to demystify official figures which place the unemployment rate at 5%, the author adds, "Inflation has oscillated between 5 and 7 percent, not the 2-3 percent disseminated. Real economic growth has been a mere 1 percent rather the 4 percent decreed."

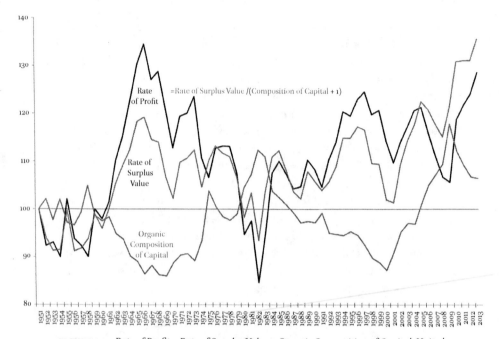

FIGURE 1   *Rate of Profit – Rate of Surplus Value – Organic Composition of Capital, United States, 1951–2013.*
SOURCE: MARCEL ROELANDTS, CAPITALISM & ECONOMIC CRISES. LAST ACCESSED 22 JUNE 2015. HTTP://WWW.CAPITALISM-AND-CRISIS.INFO/EN

As can be seen, the relation between the rate of profit, surplus value, and the organic composition of capital in the context of the US economy (still the centre of the global imperialist system) led to the revitalisation of the rate of profit between 2001 and 2004, which had fallen strongly in the previous period (1997–2001) after a major boom from 1991–1997. Beginning in 2005, however, the rate of profit began to decline once again, prefiguring the structural crisis of 2007–08. Figure 2 illustrates a variety of interrelated phenomena that, in the final years of the 2000s, pulled the United States economy and its world of labour into a scenario approximating the regime of labour super-exploitation that has dominated in dependent economies.

In this sense, Marcel Roelandts concludes that, during the period 1982–2013,

> [t]he rate of surplus value rebounded strongly following 1982 as productivity gains recovered—but without reaching the levels of the immediate post-war [period] [...] while working times were no longer decreasing, the rise of real wages slowed considerably. This recovery of the rate of surplus value, as well as the decrease of the organic composition of capital

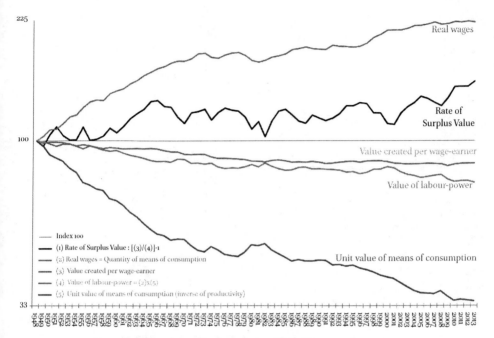

FIGURE 2   *Rate of surplus value and its determinants, United States, 1948–2013.*
            Value is calculated in labour-time
            SOURCE: ROELANDTS, CAPITALISM & ECONOMIC CRISES

(following the recovery of productivity gains after 1982), would be the basis of the rise of the rate of profit.[65]

We can infer from Figure 2 that, while the growth of real wages has slowed and remained practically stalled in the United States since the mid-1970s (where the standard of living has only managed to keep up due to longer working hours and higher levels of household debt, thanks also to the addition of women to the labour market),[66] the value of labour power (corresponding to the purchasing power of consumer goods and services) has fallen since the eighties; a growing gap expressed in the deterioration of the cost of living index (basic basket) and real purchasing power of wages. This fall in the value of labour power has been accompanied simultaneously by a reduction of the socially-necessary labour time required to produce the means of production, as can be seen in Figure 3 in the curve corresponding to the "value of the means of production."

---

65   Roelandts, Marcel, Capitalism & Economic Crises. Last accessed 22 June 2015. http://www.capitalism-and-crisis.info/en.

66   Ian J. Seda-Irizarry, "Estados Unidos y la crisis capitalista" (entrevista a Richard Wolff), *Rebelión*, 2 August 2010, accessed 7 March 2015, http://www.rebelion.org/noticia.php?id=110683.

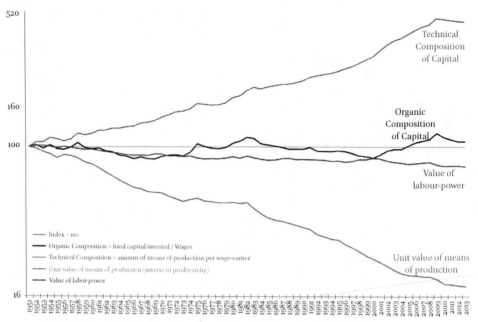

520

160

100

16

- Index = 100
- Organic Composition = fixed capital invested / Wages
- Technical Composition = amount of means of production per wage-earner
- Unit value of means of production (inverse of productivity)
- Value of labor-power

Technical
Composition
of Capital

Organic
Composition
of Capital

Value of
labour-power

Unit value of means
of production

FIGURE 3   *Organic composition of capital and its determinants, United States, 1951–2013.*
Value is calculated in labour-time
SOURCE: ROELANDTS, CAPITALISM & ECONOMIC CRISES

Despite taking place in what is still the most productive labour system of the most powerful economy in the world (albeit interacting with the global capitalism system), this movement has also reverberated throughout other advanced capitalist and dependent countries. It is in this sense, according to the results of a study in Mexico, that nt (the number of hours in the working day allotted to wages) fell from 3.24 hours in 1976, to 0.12 hours in 2006; in Spain, it fell from 4.25 hours to 2.15 hours over the same period; in Italy, from 4.30 to 2.30 hours; and lastly, in Brazil, from 3.20 to 0.12 hours.[67] By way of contrast, the same source reveals that the surplus labour time (st) appropriated by capital in the form of surplus value in Mexico was 4.38 hours in 1976, and that it increased to 7.84 hours in 2006; in Spain, it increased from 3.35 hours in the first year to 5.54 hours in 2004; in Italy, capital appropriated 3.30 hours in 1976 and 5.30 hours in 2004; while in Brazil, the number of hours appropriated went from 4.40 hours in the first year to 7.84 hours in 2004. It is clear that, due to a series of circumstances (different levels of

---

67   Luis Lozano *et al.*, *De llantas y atropellos. Trabajo, salario, productividad y derechos labo-
      rales en la industria llantera mexicana* (Mexico: Centro de Análisis Multidisciplinario –
      Universidad Nacional Autónoma de México [CAM-UNAM], Sindicato Nacional de
      Trabajadores de General Tire de México, 2009), 222 et seq.

productivity and the organic composition of capital, wage levels, rates of inflation, the strength and level of union organisation, the role of the State in the
economy and in society), the rates of exploitation and appropriation of surplus
value were higher in the dependent countries (Mexico and Brazil) than in the
developed ones (Italy, Spain). This reduction of nt has become readily visible in
Brazil over the past few decades. One of the most robust examples is the fall in
the time necessary to buy the basic market basket which, in 2009, reached its
lowest level in terms of working hours since 1970, according to the Inter-union
Department of Statistics and Socioeconomic Study (DIEESE).[68] This figure represents the exact opposite, for example, of what Mexico has experienced, where
the State has taken over three decades to drive down real wages.[69]

As we have argued, there is a drive to standardise rates of labour exploitation
by various means, ranging from the super-exploitation of labour in advanced
capitalism with the decline (or slowing) of the growth rates of real wages
and benefits to workers, to increasing working time during the workweek and
intensity of labour, as expressed (amongst other things) in the fact that the
average number of machines operated by employee went from one during
the post-war period to the current five.

In this survey, a "normal working day" is considered to be eight hours of
work, when in practice (above all in dependent countries and in certain sectors of advanced countries) it reaches up to 12 or 14 hours a day, something that
the data in Table 9 underestimates. It nonetheless clearly illustrates the degree
of exploitation and appropriation of surplus value that prevails in the global
world of labour, and to great effect in dependent countries where labour super-
exploitation operates as an additional source of accumulation.

Even in countries where labour exploitation should be relatively low due to
the supposedly democratic social and political dispositions of the population,
exploitation has increased exponentially, as illustrated in Figure 4. This graph
clearly illustrates that there is not always a positive correlation between 'progressive' governments (as governments such as the MAS in Bolivia are often
called) and the socio-economic conditions of workers, which appear to be
independent of current public policies. As can be seen, during the period prior
to the Morales government (2000–2005), the price of the basic food basket
(CNA) and the purchasing power of wages maintained a certain balance at
the height of the period of oligarchical governments; while in the period following 2006 under a supposedly popular and progressive government, the link
between the two categories was severed, to the degree that,

---

68   Alianza Global Jus Semper, "Gráficas," 17.
69   Alianza Global Jus Semper, "Gráficas."

TABLE 9   *Rates of exploitation and appropriation of surplus value in dependent and developed countries, 1976–2006*

Countries	Year	Hours Allotted to Wages	Hours Appropriated by Capital
Mexico	1976	3.24	4.38
	2006	0.12	7.48
Brazil	1976	3.20	4.40
	2004	0.12	7.48
Spain	1976	4.25	3.35
	2004	2.15	5.45
Italy	1976	4.30	3.30
	2004	2.30	5.30

SOURCE: LOZANO, 2009, P. 222

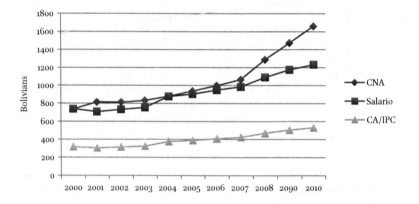

CNA (*Canasta Normativa Alimentaria*) is the basic food basket developed and updated by the Centro de Estudios para el Desarrollo Laboral y Agrario (La Paz)

Salary is the mathematical average over the average wages of "specialised workers" and "other workers" in the private sector

CA/IPC (*Canasta Alimentaria/Índice de Precious al Consumidor*) = (Basic Food Basket/Consumer Price Index)

FIGURE 4   *Bolivia: Average salary and basic food basket, 2000–2010.*
SOURCE: CARLOS ARZE VARGAS, "AUMENTO SALARIAL: ¿GARANTIZAR LA REPRODUC-CIÓN DE LA FUERZA DE TRABAJO O EL AUMENTO DE LA EXPLOTACIÓN?" *REBELIÓN*, 22 APRIL 2011, ACCESSED 8 MARCH 2015, HTTP://WWW.REBELION.ORG/DOCS/126780.PDF [ORIGINALLY PUBLISHED IN LA PAZ: CENTRO DE ESTUDIOS PARA EL DESARROLLO LABORAL Y AGRARIO, 2010]

...while in 2004 the average wage was more than 99 percent of the basket, in 2010 the average salary represented only 74 percent of the value of the CAN, revealing that a great deterioration had taken place in workers' income.[70]

This is certainly a clear example of the super-exploitation of workers in the private sector who are no longer able to cover their basic needs in terms of food, health, transportation, housing, and who no longer take part in education and recreation which, in turn, results in greater marginalisation, poverty and even further exploitation. Keeping in mind national specificities, it can be expected that this situation is also taking place in other countries of Latin America and the Caribbean.

In other parts of the world the situation is not much different. In Bangladesh, for example, workers of the 4,500 textile factories producing clothes for transnational companies like Wal-Mart, H&M and Levi Strauss receive salaries of 3000 takas (or US$43) per month. In this country, the textile sector represents 80 percent of annual exports that, in 2009, amounted to some US$16.2 billion. More than 85 percent of the total 3 million workers exploited in these factories are women who, following the global trend, receive much lower wages. In Romania, with a total workforce of around 4.84 million, 73.3 percent (or 3,546,720 people) earn less than €420 a month (or €14 a day); this in a country where the average gross salary is approximately €463 per month.[71] Foreign investment has increased day by day, originating from Austria (€9.186 million), the Netherlands (€8.402 million), Germany (€7.509 million), France (€4.295 million), Italy (€3.585 million) and Spain (€604 million), according to data from the Romanian National Bank.[72] Finally, in the Sri Lankan textile industry (the most important sector of the economy), the current basic salary is around US$80 a month, which, together with the income earned through overtime, may reach US$115, according to Lalitha Ranjini Kumari of the National Workers Union. A dignified wage, on the other hand, would need to reach around US$180 a month.[73]

---

70   Arze, "Aumento salarial," 6.

71   Ministry of Labour, Family & Social Protection of Romania, cited in José Luis Forneo, "Un 35% de los asalariados rumanos ganan menos de 170 euros netos al mes," *Rebelión*, 26 March 2011, accessed 8 March 2015, http://www.rebelion.org/noticia.php?id=125139.

72   "Un 35% de los asalariados rumanos ganan menos de 170 euros netos al mes," *Un vallekano en Rumania Blog*, 24 March 2011, accessed 30 April 2015, http://imbratisare.blogspot.co .uk/2011/03/en-2010-un-35-de-los-rumanos-ganaban.html.

73   Feizal Samath, "Industria de la vestimenta corteja a mujeres," *Rebelión*, 13 February 2011, accessed 8 March 2015, http://www.rebelion.org/noticia.php?id=122341.

Wages and Labour Productivity

The issue of the relation between wages and productivity is very important to the objectives of our study. A decline in wages and productivity has been seen in every region (with the exception of Asia) due to the inability of companies to pay higher wages. If the level of the workforce is maintained, the utility and wages of active workers will be affected, and so companies opt instead to reduce employment.[74] In its Global Wage Report 2010/11, the ILO notes that over the long term wages have tended to count for a smaller share in OECD countries since the mid-eighties.[75] The causes of the decline are attributed to the following factors: 1) the introduction of new technology; 2) the effects of globalisation; 3) the increased influence of financial institutions; and 4) a weakening of labour market institutions. In addition, the report indicates that increased openness to trade has the effect of moderating wage increases. It concludes that

> ...it is plausible that the four factors are correlated with each other. For instance, technological change, globalisation and the restructuring of the economy tend to go hand in hand. For this reason, it is often difficult to isolate the net effect of each factor on the wage share.[76]

The ILO notes the existence of a low-wage structure that results in low pay and wage instability, and where 66 percent of workers earn less than two-thirds of the median wage of all jobs.[77] The reality is that over the last 15 years, in the majority of countries (including those of advanced capitalism), low wage jobs and *precarious employment* have tended to rise which is insufficient to reproduce the value of labour power under normal conditions of the worker and his or her family (what the ILO calls 'decent work'). Thus a new profile of workers in low-wage jobs has taken shape mainly characterised by 1) low levels of education; 2) youth; 3) women (the universal characteristic of labour markets), whose average monthly income currently represents around 75 percent of the

---

74   ILO, *Global Wage Report 2010/11: Wage Policies in Times of Crisis* (Geneva: Interna tional Labour Office, 2010), 18, accessed 8 March 2015, http://www.ilo.org/wcmsp5/ groups/public/---dgreports/ -dcomm/---publ/documents/publication/wcms_145265 .pdf.

75   ILO, *Global Wage*, 25.

76   ILO, *Global Wage*, 26.

77   ILO, *Global Wage*, 31.

average wage received by men;[78] and 4) members of minority ethnic, racial, or immigrant groups.[79]

Low wages, precariousness, and high rates of extensive and intensive exploitation have increased the risks of unemployment and poverty, and for most populations, pulled them away from the possibility of reaching the so-called Millennium Goals and 'decent work.' Thus, in 2007 (before the current economic crisis), 79 million people in the European Union were estimated to be at risk of falling into poverty and another 32 million were already in that status, out of a total working population of 218,451,000. In the same year, an estimated 17.5 million workers currently working would be hit by poverty, while 8 percent of the unemployed in the 27 members of the European Union received an income below the poverty line.[80]

> [S]ince the mid-1990s, the proportion of people on low pay—defined as less than two-thirds of median wages—has increased in more than two-thirds of the countries for which data are available. This includes countries such as Argentina, China, Germany, Indonesia, Ireland, the Republic of Korea, Poland and Spain. In these and other countries with high or growing rates of low page, there is a risk that a large number of people will feel left behind.[81]

In Spain, for example, labour inspectors have observed that immigrant workers who work in restaurants and internet cafés in Barcelona often do so without access to a contract or social security. Others work in companies that operate without a business license or, where they did, for another kind of business. They also discovered the case of seventy-one immigrant employees of a citrus farm in Castellón, Valencia, who received wages under the legal minimum while living in three houses provided for them for €120 per month. In Elda, Alicante, twenty workers were discovered to be working for a shoe company without an employment contract and social security, from whom they

---

78   ILO, *Global Wage*, 45. Spain is the fourth European country to show a major wage break between men and women, behind Austria, the United Kingdom and Slovakia, according to Eurostat. Cited in Adecco & International Research Centre on Organizations-IESE Business School, "Con un 34,4%, España es el cuarto país europeo con mayor brecha salarial entre hombres y mujeres," 1 January 2010, accessed 13 March 2015, http://www.adecco.es/_data/NotasPrensa/pdf/197.pdf.

79   ILO, *Global Wage*, 37, 41.

80   ILO, *Global Wage*, 47.

81   ILO, *Global Wage*, 79–80.

were owed a monthly allowance.[82] Overall, this situation of indiscriminate exploitation of workers by large firms from rich countries such as Nike, Wal-Mart, El Corte Inglés, Stradivarius, Zara and Lafayette has only intensified with the frequent and widespread use of outsourcing, which taps into massive economic and labour-related advantages made available by virtually every country and, above all by underdeveloped countries. One of the most pressing consequences, notes Richard Sennett, is that "...the shift of work to low-wage sites around the world drags down wages in advanced economies like the United States,"[83] contrary to what certain corporate bureaucracies from this country believe.

It is key here to investigate the essence of the mechanism of labour super-exploitation in dependent economies, to determine the trajectories of real wages of workers in advanced capitalism (in terms of the value of labour power and inflation), and to also clarify the trend towards the increase of working time, above all in the countries of southern Europe which have been hit hard by the crisis, as well as by austerity measures imposed by big capital and the State. In this sense, Marini writes,

> ...the superexploitation of labour which implies (as we have seen) that the value of labour power is not [fully] remunerated, entails the reduction of the consumption capacity of workers and restricts the possibility of realising these goods. Superexploitation is reflected in a wage scale whose average level is to be found below the value of the workforce, which implies that even those layers of workers whose pay reaches above the average value of labour power (skilled workers, technicians, etc.) see their wages constantly pushed downwards, dragged down by the regulatory role that the average wages plays with respect to the scale of wages overall.[84]

As clarified here, wages in dependent capitalism fluctuate around an average wage that amounts to less than the value of labour power. At the same time, wage hierarchies tend to equal this average, or to fluctuate below or above it. It is clear that the presence of labour super-exploitation can in no way be removed from the economic structures and capitalist dynamics of the imperialist countries. The structures of wage hierarchies, in addition to being influenced by productivity, are overdetermined by productive and labour processes

---

82   Enric Llopis, "La economía sumergida se dispara con la crisis," *Rebelión*, 12 August 2011, accessed 13 March 2015, http://www.rebelion.org/noticia.php?id=133888.

83   Sennett, *Corrosion*, 127.

84   Marini, "El ciclo," 53.

based on the dynamic of relative surplus value and also on official state policies around wages, labour relations, unions and social welfare. If, as we have
suggested, wages in the advanced countries (which, for example, are higher in
England, the Netherlands and Canada than in the United States) are governed
by relative surplus value—in contrast to dependent countries—it is the latter
which determines the possibilities and scope for reducing workers' real wages,
punishing their consumption (or conversely, not) in this way. This would be
the line of demarcation between the distinct forms and concrete methods that
super-exploitation takes in the advanced capitalist economies.

In Table 10, the gross annual wage in the European Union can be seen listed
by country, distinguishing those who fall above the average of the union from
those who fall below. Of course, we do not have enough information to determine whether the amount corresponding to this average falls above, is equal
to, or is below the value of labour power.

TABLE 10   *Annual gross average wage (€) in the European Union for full-time employees, 2008*

Country	Amount
United Kingdom	46,056 (+70 percent of the average)
The Netherlands	42,720
Germany[85]	40,914
Belgium	39,343
Austria	38,622
Sweden	36,186
Finland	36,128
France	32,867
EU Average	27,036
Spain	21,500
Portugal	17,179
Hungary	9,899
Slovakia	8,353
Romania	5,479
Bulgaria	2862 (-90 percent of the average)

SOURCE: EUROSTAT (2008), IN ADECCO & INTERNATIONAL RESEARCH CENTRE ON
ORGANIZATIONS-IESE BUSINESS SCHOOL

85   The gross average salary of a German full-time employee in the industrial sector rose to
3,256 euros per month in this period, while those of service sector workers were on average 3,211 euros.

While the reduction of real wages below the actual value of labour power is not yet apparent in advanced capitalist countries, there is evidence of this occurring hierarchically in the world of work in the countries most affected by the crisis such as Greece, Spain, Portugal, Ireland and others which now make up the grouping of countries categorised in this book under the label of new peripheries (referring to those countries making up the former socialist bloc led by the extinct Soviet Union). But there is evidence that, since the nineties (and even before), the consumption levels of the population of the advanced countries have been deteriorating under the influence of public policies and the crisis, which have severely punished the employment and income of workers. In the North, the compression of spending levels has been further exacerbated by the deregulation of the labour market: the de-indexation of earnings, part-time employment, early retirement and the imposition of so-called 'voluntary' wage cuts. In turn, the practice of attrition (which shifts the social burden of unemployment onto the younger age groups) has barred an entire generation from the job-market.[86]

The *Global Wage Report 2010/11* reveals that the economic crisis since 2008 has increased open unemployment to around 200 million people globally, a level never before recorded, while other contingents of workers have withdrawn from the workforce altogether. As one can imagine, this expanded industrial reserve army has had a direct impact on labour exploitation, forcing down wages and at the same time, intensifying competition between workers themselves and thus, undoubtedly, resulting in favourable returns on capital investment which, in the midst of the crisis of 2008–2010, saw increasing profits located in the exterior.[87] Real wages have also suffered major losses in purchasing power. In this way, the global average growth rate of real wages from 2008 to 2009 was reduced by half (in comparison to earlier years), thereby affecting the purchasing power and social security of those who had been able to maintain their jobs. And it can be said with certainty that the deterioration of wages and purchasing power will continue to the extent that the crisis, and the imposition of adjustment and austerity policies, deepens in European countries; as well as in the United States, which has found itself on the brink of recession with open unemployment in excess of 10 percent. To a large extent, this situation can be explained by a real disconnect between economic cycles in the United States (growth, recession, depression,

---

86   Chossudovsky, *Globalisation*, 82.
87   Claudio Katz, "Discusiones sobre el declive de Estados Unidos," *Rebelión*, 30 July 2011, accessed 14 March 2015, http://www.rebelion.org/noticia.php?id=133194.

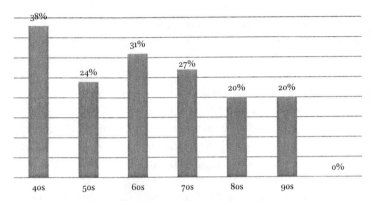

FIGURE 5   *United States: Job growth by decade as a percentage of active workers*
            SOURCE: NEIL IRWIN, "AUGHTS WERE A LOST DECADE FOR U.S. ECON-
            OMY, WORKERS." WASHINGTON POST, 2 JANUARY 2010, CITED IN FRED
            GOLDSTEIN, "CAPITALISM," 23

crisis), and processes of job creation which have been practically nil over the
past decade, readily observable in Figure 5 above.

The severity of the crisis has also manifested in the growing disconnect
between wages and labour productivity; a wage inequality at the very heart of
advanced capitalist countries, and in the low wages of approximately 330 million people still employed globally but in conditions very far from 'decent
work.' The ILO has drawn attention to two historical periods in the trajectory of
wages: first, a favourable period between 1995 and 2007, and the period that
followed, which has been characterised by a strong economic reversal not seen
since the Great Depression of the 1930s. A fundamental part of the latter period
corresponded to the real estate and financial crisis in the United States starting
from the prolonged recession that began in December 2007, after economic
expansion that lasted more than seventy months from November 2001. But
despite the supposed economic recovery in 2010, according to the ILO, uncertainty still reigns and prospects are bleak for the near future, sending almost
daily shivers throughout every stock exchange in the world.

The global unemployment rate grew from 5.7 percent of the global workforce in 2007 to 6.4 percent in 2009, representing an addition of around
30 million people to the ranks of the unemployed. The estimated total number
of unemployed increased from around 178 million people in 2007 to 206.7 million in 2009, reflecting increases in the workforce, wage levels, the number of
hours worked, and quality of work of workers in advanced societies. Meanwhile,
in the underdeveloped and dependent countries, the crisis manifested itself in
a deterioration of the quality of work and in an expressed transition towards

'more vulnerable' forms of work.[88] Of the total economically active population in advanced countries, 86 percent are wage workers while the figure is 35 percent in Asia and less than 30 percent in Africa. In the first setting, the division of the working population between men and women is approximately equal, while in the latter the female workforce fell notably in relation to that of men, particularly in South Asia and sub-Saharan Africa.

We turn to the main wage trends identified by the ILO in order to assess its impact on the formation of productive structures and regimes based on super-exploitation. Including China, which accounts for over half of the total wage labour in Asia, the global real monthly wage grew 2.8 percent in 2007, 1.5 percent in 2008, and 1.6 percent in 2009.[89] In China alone, wages grew by 13.1 percent in 2007, 11.7 percent in 2008, and 12.8 percent in 2009, contrary to predictions that there would be a steady deterioration of wages in that country. What stands out for the international organisation is that global figures are strongly influenced by wage dynamics in China, without which the global trend in the growth rate of wages would be corrected downwards to stand at 2.2 percent in 2007, 0.8 percent in 2008 and 0.7 percent in 2009. On the other hand, in the G20 (including China), the real monthly wage increased 2.8 percent in 2007, 1.5 percent in 2008 and 1.7 percent in 2009. Without China, these figures fall to 1.8 percent in the first year, 0.5 percent in the second, and 0.5 percent in the third respectively. Wages stayed virtually stagnant throughout the crisis and saw spikes to the price of necessary consumer goods for the reproduction of labour power. Of course, it remains an open question as to whether this pattern will improve with the 'overcoming' of the crisis; whether it is just a temporary situation as some analysts suggest, or whether it is a structural, long-term situation which will sooner or later impact the hierarchies found at the top of the wage pyramid, as we believe.

The ILO recognises that the growth of wages at the global level decelerated throughout the 2008–09 crisis due, in large measure, to inflation which obviously affected the purchasing power and living standards of the great mass of the population, with a strong impact in Germany, England, the United States and Canada (see Table 11). "Altogether, the level of real wages fell in 12 of the 28 advanced countries in 2008 and in seven of the advanced countries in 2009," which also saw negative growth rates in this period; above all, in the United States where purchasing power was also affected by increased inflation.[90] In Latin America

---

88   The ILO is incapable of recognizing that these "vulnerable" forms are in reality precarious and marked by labour super-exploitation.

89   ILO, *Global Wage*, 4, 12.

90   ILO, *Global Wage*, 6.

TABLE 11   *Cumulative wage growth by region in percentages (1999=100)*

Country	1999	2006	2007	2008	2009
Advanced countries	100	104.2	105.0	104.5	105.2
Central & Eastern Europe	100	144.8	154.4	161.4	161.3
Eastern Europe & Central Asia	100	264.1	308.9	341.6	334.1
Asia	100	168.8	180.9	193.8	209.3
Latin America & the Caribbean	100	106.7	110.3	112.4	114.8
Africa	100	111.2	112.8	113.4	116.1
Middle East	100	101.9	102.4	–	–
Global	100	115.6	118.9	120.7	122.6

SOURCE: ILO, *GLOBAL WAGE REPORT 2010/11*, 15

and the Caribbean, real wages were reduced by 3.3 percent in 2007, 1.9 percent in 2008, ending up at 2.2 percent in 2009. This trend had a strong effect on wage patterns in Brazil, which is home to about 39 percent of wage workers in the region (see Table 11). As a result,

> ...global average wages increased by almost one-quarter over this period. This increase was driven by developing regions such as Asia, where wages have more than doubled since 1999, or countries in Eastern Europe and Central Asia where wages more than tripled (which partly reflects the depth of the wage decline in the 1990s). By comparison, real wages grew only modestly in Latin America and the Caribbean, in Africa and in the Middle East. In advanced countries, real wages increased by only about 5 per cent in real terms over the whole decade, reflecting a period of wage moderation.[91]

This period of 'wage moderation,' as the ILO euphemistically calls it, should be subject to future investigation in order to determine whether the phenomenon in fact remains a decisive feature of wages or, rather, whether it will be turned around when, at some point, the current crisis of the capitalist mode of production

---

91   ILO, *Global Wage*, 14.

is overcome. But the optimism of the ILO shows its limits when it then states that,

> ...it is plausible that along with persistently high unemployment, there will be continued (or even stronger) pressures on wages in the coming years of economic recovery and, in this case, the full impact of the crisis on wages may yet remain to be seen.[92]

We are clearly already witnessing a wage scenario in which purchasing power has been slashed, larger numbers of low-wage workers are to be found in the context of enormously precarious work, and where increasing social and contractual rights have been lost. The structural crisis of capitalism is now seeking to 'recover' itself through cuts in public spending, particularly by cutting social spending and intensifying the dismantling of the welfare state which flourished in the post-war period in the central countries of advanced capitalism.

Neoliberalism, Austerity and Labour Super-exploitation in Advanced Capitalism

The low costs of labour power in the international sphere have permitted the lowering of production costs in Third World countries while, at the same time, curbing the growth of the metropoles of advanced capitalism. In addition, another trend in play sees the incorporation of technology in productive processes and hence, a revaluing of labour power as the source of extraordinary profits.[93] All of this has given rise to a deterioration of the social existence of wage workers, for example, in Europe, where working and living conditions are becoming worse; to finance their debts and budget deficits, European governments "have had to cut back spending programs, lower public employment

---

92   ILO, *Global Wage*, 79.

93   In this context, neoclassical economic theory has been resurrected that (following David Ricardo and neoclassical authors such as Eli Heckscher and Bertil Ohlin) proposes the theory of 'comparative costs' which posits that a country must specialise and export those products whose production enjoys sufficient resources. To this end, sufficient cheap manpower is required to produce 'comparative advantages' derived from the costs of production. In other words, it must specialise in the export of goods produced with abundant cheap labour in exchange for products imported from countries that have an abundance of capital. Obviously this to some extent traces the famous centre-periphery theory of ECLAC.

and wages, and charge more for public services, from medical care to educa-tion."[94] Currently, countries facing problems with their so-called 'sovereign debt' (bonds issued by the national government in foreign currency) as a per-centage of their Gross Domestic Product (GDP) include Ireland (with 96.2 per-cent), Greece (142.8 percent), Portugal (93.0 percent), Spain (60.1 percent), Italy (119 percent), Belgium (96.8 percent), and Austria (72.3 percent). Generally, the eurozone has an accumulative debt of 70 percent of its cumulative GDP in a context of weak economic growth, moderate inflation, increased unemploy-ment and the extension of poverty as the result of job loss.[95]

This is the current reality for a good part of the European Union. Greece, with youth unemployment at more than 40 percent of the working age popula-tion and with poor employment prospects, stands out in the European con-text.[96] The programme approved by its parliament on 29 July 2011 (more than a year after Greece received €110 billion, or US$159, from the European Union and International Monetary Fund to deal with the supposedly 'Greek' crisis) empowered the government, amidst a wave of social protest and demonstra-tions by workers and people more generally, to immediately implement decisions that would have a strong social impact. This took place under the directives of a five-year austerity plan meant to 'save' €28,400 million, plus more than €50,000 by way of privatisations (of the main producer of electricity as well as firms from sectors such as telecommunications, the lottery, airports and natu-ral gas). We highlight a few key points from this austerity plan:

- In 2011, taxes would increase by €2.32 billion; in 2012, by €3.38 billion; in 2013, €152 million and €699 million in 2014, naturally taken from the pocket of the taxpayer.
- Solidarity tax. The State plans to raise €1,300 million through a so-called 'soli-darity tax,' which would impose rates (between 1 and 5 percent) proportional

---

94   Michel Husson, "Breakup of the Eurozone?" *Counterpunch*, 27–29 May 2011, accessed
      23 March 2015, http://www.counterpunch.org/2011/05/27/breakup-of-the-eurozone/.
95   "Secuelas de la crisis golpean hoy a Europe," *El Universal*, 11 July 2011, accessed 23 March
      2015, http://www.eluniversal.com.mx/notas/780376.html.
96   "Contrary to some media reports, workers in Greece work longer hours than in Germany
      (an average 2,161 hours annually per worker in 2009, as opposed to 1,382 in Germany).
      Furthermore, hourly labour productivity increased more than twice as fast in Greece as in
      Germany in the ten years after the euro was introduced (26.3% in Greece compared with
      11.6% in Germany)." Marcia Frangakis, "How the EU Made the Greek Crisis Worse,"
      Counterpunch, 15-17 July 2011, accessed 23 March 2015, http://www.counterpunch
      .org/2011/07/15/how-the-eu-made-the-greek-crisis-worse/.

to income. The threshold for tax contributions would fall from €12,000 to 8,000.

- Increased value-added tax. Bars and restaurants would increase the VAT rate from 13 to 23 percent immediately. Taxes raised on luxury goods would also rise.
- Privatisations. The State plans to raise €50 billion by 2015 from the sale of state assets; amongst others, by breaking up the monopolies in gambling, postal services and port operators of Piraeus and Thessaloniki.
- Cuts to the public sector. Cuts of €770 million have been planned for 2011, €600 million in 2012, €448 million in 2013, €300 million in 2014 and €71 million for 2015, through the reduction of public sector workers, cuts to pensions and the termination of temporary contracts.
- Reduction of benefits. €5 billion less have been allocated to social benefits and social security contributions, and there will be a crackdown on tax evasion amongst informal workers and those working at undeclared jobs.[97]

In this way,

> [t]he countries of the European periphery, with much lower productivity than central countries, and without the ability to devalue their currencies due to their being linked to the euro, are intent on compensating for these deficits by increasing exports that they judge to be feasible, thanks to the internal depreciation of labour incorporated in such goods; that is, increasing the rates of exploitation. In Spain, it increased from 0.7 in the mid-1950s (under the Franco regime) to just over 0.9 by the end of the millennium. This is an increase of almost 100 percent, which means that for every 8 hours of work, 4 are carried out for the employer. Moreover, according to Eurostat, full-time wage workers work an average

97 "Grecia aprueba los recortes y libera el camino para recibir la ayuda de la UE y el FMI," *El País*, 29 June 2011, accessed 24 March 2015, http://economia.elpais.com/economia/2011/06/29/actualidad/1309332773_850215.html. See also "El Parlamento griego apoya las nuevas medidas de austeridad," *La Jornada*, 22 June 2011, accessed 24 March 2015, http://www.jornada.unam.mx/2011/06/22/economia/034n2eco. The most serious factor that will exacerbate the crisis in Greece is that, following the recent parliamentary approval of a programme to save up to 78 billion euros ("with which the country will fulfil the requirements to continue receiving aid," according to the international press), they are now working to secure a second bailout of up to 120 billion euros. Please see my analysis of the Greek crisis in, "Grecia: preludio de la crisis global del capital," *Rebelión*, 16 May 2011, accessed 24 March 2015, http://www.rebelion.org/noticia.php?id=105954.

of 8.5 hours extra per week, of which 4.7 hours of overtime are not paid for; which means that almost 10 percent of the regular workweek agreed to by convention is given away to the boss.[98]

The austerity plans to save the collapse of big European capital have been very similar across Europe, due to their original elaboration by the International Monetary Fund (IMF), the European Bank for International Settlements and the neoliberal governments of the region, with the vast experience in the impoverishment and submission of peoples of dependent countries that the international bodies representing the interests of big transnational capital have. The president of the European Central Bank, for example, Jean-Claude Trichet, urged governments to reduce their public deficits and required them to 'save' up to €25 billion from 2011 to 2013. Before buying bonds from distressed economies like Italy and Spain, he encouraged the latter to implement more severe measures, including facilitating layoffs, pension and healthcare reform, increasing taxes and the VAT, and setting in motion plans to privatise public sector enterprises.

In this way, the Greek crisis spread like a whirlwind to other countries like England, where the conservative Prime Minister, David Cameron (supported by the opposition Labour Party) defended cuts to the social budget and increasing tuition fees, causing a genuinely popular uprising in such cities as London, Birmingham and others. In Italy, following the lowering of the rating of Italy's sovereign debt from stable to negative over several months by the ratings agency Standard & Poor's, and with economic growth at around zero, in July 2011 the Senate approved a severe austerity plan which, among other things, included cuts of more than €79 billion, with the intention to correct a deficit that had risen to 120 percent of GDP (€1.9 billion), in addition to introducing reductions to social spending, healthcare and education, and the gradual increase of the retirement age for women to 65 years beginning in 2015. The government declared its willingness to introduce reforms to modify the labour market and to undertake the privatisation of public services in accordance with the requirements of other European countries and the European Central Bank.[99] Amongst the austerity measures, citizens have been obliged to pay more for some public health services, as well as to increase their tax contributions on

---

98 Andrés Piqueras, "Cuando la 'guerra de clase' se hace guerra en los campos de batalla," *Rebelión*, 12 May 2011, accessed 24 March 2015, http://www.rebelion.org/noticia .php?id=128167.

99 "En peligro, la economía mundial: Zoellick," *La Jornada*, 14 August 2011, accessed 24 March 2015, http://www.jornada.unam.mx:8810/2011/08/14/economia/027n1eco.

pensions that exceed €90,000 annually. The plan set out cuts in the sectors of healthcare, social welfare, education, housing and regional budgets; in addition for 2014, it sought to reduce the public deficit to zero.[100] In the area of healthcare alone, the Italians have had to pay €25 for each emergency service for 'non-serious' illnesses (and who knows how much more, if they are deemed to be serious!), and €10 for the attention of a public sector specialist. According to estimates published in the local press at the time, the adjustment plan was set to cost between €500-1,000 per family each year in healthcare tickets, new and higher taxes, increased retirement age and restrictions around state contributions to the family.

Turning to the foreign debt crisis of the most powerful economy on the planet, on 1 August 2011 President Barack Obama signed and issued an agreement (with approval from the House of Representatives) that would elevate the US debt ceiling by US$2.1 billion over the following ten years, with the goal of 'liberating' resources and reversing the threat of a default that would have put the global economy (including its main creditors, like China) in jeopardy. The new law would bring the foreign debt from US$14.3 billion to the astronomical sum of US$16.4 billion (or 102 percent of GDP).[101] The second phase of the law, which would make $900 billion available to the Treasury Department to cover payment obligations to US creditors, promised to reduce the federal deficit by approximately an additional 1.2 billion dollars through social spending cuts totalling $2.4 billion over the next decade in the areas of education, healthcare, food and infrastructure. Significantly, following the intervention and demand of the Republicans, the law did not establish a mandate to raise taxes on the rich and North American corporations, but did so rather in relation to the rural and urban working classes.[102]

While these growing challenges and (national and international) contradictions have led some to speak of a 'crisis of hegemony,' this new economic reality confirms that the only way to try to overcome (but not to resolve) the

---

100 "Italia golpea a los más débiles para reducir su déficit en 79.000 millones," *El País*, 15 July 2011, accessed 24 March 2015, http://elpais.com/diario/2011/07/15/economia/1310680806_850215.html.

101 Economist Intelligence Unit, "Estados Unidos: ¿fin de la crisis?" *La Jornada*, 9 August 2011, accessed 24 March 2015, http://www.jornada.unam.mx/2011/08/09/economia/030n1eco.

102 See "Obama promulga ley para evitar suspensión de pagos," *El Universal*, 2 August 2011, accessed 24 March 2015, http://www.eluniversal.com.mx/notas/783126.html; "El Senado de Estados Unidos aprueba la subida del techo de deuda para evitar la quiebra," *El País*, 2 August 2011, accessed 24 March 2015, http://internacional.elpais.com/internacional/2011/08/02/actualidad/1312236006_850215.html.

structural crisis of capitalism is to demand additional surplus labour from the working population by doubling rates of exploitation and introducing cuts to wages and social benefits (including pensions), increasing the retirement age, increasing taxation rates, a reduction in global consumption, enabling higher household debt, as well as seeing through strong declines in the consumption fund of the population.

The neoliberal exit for big capital and the North American government is condemned to fail sooner or later by virtue of the fact that it relies fundamentally on strengthening the interests of the parasitic fractions of finance and speculative capital; and in so far as it does not provide solutions and structural reform at least favourable to productive capital which could result (with reformist policies) in job creation, in rising real wages and incentives for internal market growth, and in the improvement of the working and living conditions of the population. And this situation has been sustained and reproduced by virtue of the pattern of accumulation of neoliberal capital which is globally hegemonic, one of whose characteristics is precisely that of being able to sustain itself through fraudulent operations and corruption. In effect,

> [f]inancial and speculative capital has taken a hegemonic, dominant position in the power bloc. It is parasitic capital that lives on speculative operations which revolve around cheating and deception; something that spills from the heights to the rest of society as a whole. In the case of neoliberalism, the slow rhythms of accumulation and growth, the penetration of imports and the destruction of that section of the industrial park that produces for the domestic market has given way to a reduction of productive sectors and of employment.[103]

The bourgeois fractions of financial and speculative capital have urged European governments to reduce their public deficits and demanded that they 'save' billions of euros through austerity measures that facilitate dismissals, pension reform, the privatisation of healthcare systems and state enterprises, and increased taxes.

According to our working thesis, this means that North American, European, and global capital is reaching a stage in the historical process of capitalist accumulation and the international division of labour that produces less value and surplus value, and therefore, which tends to punish rates of profit and to offset its losses by elevating the financial deficits of the State (as we have seen

---

103   José Carlos Valenzuela Feijóo, *Sociología de la corrupción. Alianzas, corrupción y conciencia de clase* [mimeo].

in the European Union). It also seeks to remedy the situation by resorting to further exploitation of labour through dismeasured increases of working time without pay, greater intensification of labour, and also through a series of austerity measures and the reduction of consumption of the population.

Conclusion

The new morphology of capitalism is grounded in labour super-exploitation, but this takes distinct forms in different countries and regions. The world today is much more complex than it was in previous decades. For this reason, labour super-exploitation in dependent countries determines the dynamic of the production of relative surplus value, regardless of any advances in the area of industrialisation, technological modernisation of productive and labour processes, or the development of agribusiness and modern mining. Meanwhile, in advanced capitalist countries that have been thrown into upheaval by the crisis and the severity of the austerity measures its governments have adopted and imposed upon its populations—in the context of its economic cycles and the maintenance of a high wage structure for certain sections of workers, coupled with the adoption of leading technology, the strength of domestic consumer markets, and the hegemonic role that the global system plays—super-exploitation as a category depends on the dynamics of producing and reproducing relative surplus value by lowering the value of labour power, and so, effecting the reduction of the costs of goods and services that constitute the consumer fund of the working population.

In this context, the new peripheries have served to support the expansion of capital investment from the major countries of the European Union, which has enabled them to lower their production costs, to capitalise on differentials in wages and professional qualifications on offer, and ultimately, to pressure other regions and countries (such as Latin America and Africa) to lower the cost of their workforce, and to serve as receptacles of their investments, taking advantage of the existence of neoliberal governments sympathetic to their interests.

Epilogue: The Future of Work

Georges Friedman, one of the founders of the sociology of work together with Pierre Naville, broadly defined the discipline as the study of human collectivities that possess a certain level of stability and permanence across time, which are constituted through work and which are necessary in order to work. This classical definition of the social sciences which, with their theoretical, meth-odological, analytical and epistemological standpoints, have configured a dimension of knowledge fundamental to understanding the essence, dynam-ics, and trends in contemporary societies, could not be more appropriate.

We define work as a philosophical, ontological, and historical category in the sense of being an *originating principle* of humanity without which one can-not even conceive the bare outlines of human life. Work under capitalism is distinct from labour in all previous societies due to the fact that it is subordi-nated to capitalist accumulation, and in so far as it has been made into a com-modity that is bought and sold like any other. Clearly, we must also emphasise that pre-capitalist societies are structured according to the essential character-istics of the capitalist mode of production in the same way as are other social communities, even when they formally exist at the margins of capitalism's main determinations and principals (such as private property, trade, exploita-tion, wage labour, and the appropriation of the products of labour by capital).

On the other hand, we argue that despite the historical changes that have taken place over the past four decades, the core of the capitalist mode of pro-duction has not changed, as the thesis on the post-industrial and post-capitalist society maintains. To the contrary, it has been extended and rescaled to those spaces, territories, populations and border regions of countries which suc-cumbed to the resounding disintegration of the Soviet Union and the socialist bloc, reinforced through the universalisation of neoliberal policies governed by the economic and strategic priorities of developed countries. In this way, the reach of capitalist accumulation and of human collectivities under its logic of production, reproduction, exchange and consumption, has spread to the extent that only with difficulty can one today locate a society, country or terri-tory untouched by the capitalist system. As Dídimo Castillo writes,

> [b]y rupturing and displacing national and regional borders, [capitalism] deterritorialised social relations and generated complex networks of mul-tiple events, characterised by the simultaneity in time, discontinuities in space.[104]

Fundamentally, this is because the system cannot exist and reproduce itself within the territorial confines set out by national borders, as occurred during its historical development in the 20th century. It needs to expand beyond these limits in order to resolve the contradictions generated by overproduction and the realisation of commodities and surplus value, as revealed by Rosa

---

104   Castillo, *Los nuevos*, 34.

Luxemburg in her work, *The Accumulation of Capital*, which challenged the schemes of reproduction of volume II of Marx's *Capital*.

What is important today is that capitalism is a globalised system that reaches practically every corner of the earth and which raises the prospect that there are no further territories, countries or communities sustained by pre-capitalist modes of production to expand into in order to guarantee the realisation of continued surplus value and profit. Rather, and as a consequence, capital realisation must take place (as supposed in *Capital*) within the system itself under its own laws and operating mechanisms. This issue has raised a series of new problems and contradictions that we have identified in this book and which speak to the underlying causes of the current crisis. Today, this crisis finds its fullest expression particularly in what we call *toxic capitalism*, which designates the great ecological destruction inherent in its operation and the destructive humiliation of the human species. Here, we find ourselves in agreement with a *Manifesto of Terrified Economists* written by four French intellectuals who have characterised the crisis as a genuine social crisis with ecological and political consequences on a global scale.[105]

We have referred to the structural problems derived from the challenge of producing value and surplus value which, in short, manifest in two interlinked phenomena. On the one hand, advanced capitalist countries (and in this context, hegemonic countries such as Germany, France, the United States, and Japan) have seen a decrease in the value of labour power corresponding to the reproduction of the working class and social categories which are reproduced on the basis of wage labour. And on the other hand, the magnitude of relative surplus value is increasingly less; while it continues to increase, it does so at a marginal pace, an issue that speaks to the stagnant or declining growth rates of these countries (e.g., Germany)[106] and, more generally, in the global economy, with the exception of countries like China and India.

The second phenomenon identified in this book is that in order to mitigate or counteract this contradiction of the global economy, big capital has directed its investments predominantly towards the financial sector and strengthened fictitious capital, which assumed hegemony in the global system during the

---

105   Philippe Askenazy, Thomas Coutrot, Henri Sterdyniak and André Orléan, *Manifeste d'économistes atterrés. Crise et dettes en Europe. Dix fausses évidences, 22 mesuresen débat pour sortir de l'impasse* (Paris: Les Liens qui Iibèient, 2010).

106   "Official sources say that the German economy, the most powerful in the European Union, has stagnated in so far as its GDP grow only 0.1 percent in the previous trimester, lower than the 0.5 percent forecast by the government and by experts." "Alemania sufre un parón en el segunda trimestre de 2011," *El País*, 16 August 2011, accessed 30 March 2015, http://economia.elpais.com/economia/2011/08/16/actualidad/1313479975_850215.html.

1980s and 1990s. For this reason, most theoretical tacks have interpreted the crisis in terms of plunging stock market values given that (in addition to the banks, investment funds, insurance and real estate companies) investments by big capital and transnational corporations have been mainly concentrated here. This, in turn, has meant that production processes have been strongly punished with a consequent reduction in jobs and increased layoffs.

Until now, this has been the strategy pursued by capital to defend its class interests in order to bypass, or mitigate, the falling rate of profit. And to all appearances, this situation will not change in either the medium or long term, given that the policies recently introduced by European Union member states have been loyal to the dictates of the International Monetary Fund and the European Bank for International Settlements (the equivalent of the central banks of the countries of the union), and thus, in keeping with the strictest application of neoliberal principles and policies.

These tendencies will provoke a search for a convenient exit that will restore the profitability of capital; a remedy predicated on recourse to greater rates of exploitation of labour power in both dependent and developed countries. But with a difference: while the mechanisms of labour super-exploitation in dependent economies dominate those of productivity and relative surplus value, in advanced capitalist countries the latter shape the former.

Having established this distinction between the two types of capitalism, we then established the tendency of super-exploitation to become generalised in the global system as a way to increase surplus value and to improve the rate of profit. To this end, recourse has been taken to prolonging the working week, increasing the intensity of work and/or by reducing the consumption fund of workers. These mechanisms may act somewhat autonomously but more usually they do so in combination with one another. The important thing is that this reality is expressed in the formation of hierarchies based on low wages, in an increasing concentration of income, and in the constitution of a precarious, segmented and flexibilised world of work, subject to labour regimes *without* social benefits such as health-care, education, housing, social previsions and job stability. Added to these categories of workers in what in Europe has been called the *social precariat*, the social and political subject mobilised against labour precariousness and super-exploitation in an effort to recover its rights and improve its living and working conditions.

Whether this can be achieved under capitalism or not is the subject of another discussion that we cannot broach here. The political and social volatility of global, regional, national, and local realities overrides any 'progressive' or reformist exit to the crisis per se. Rather, the crisis is intensifying and multiplying in direct confrontation with capital, which tends to react with the most extreme violence against popular and workers' movements when cornered.

References

Adecco and International Research Centre on Organizations – IESE Business School. "Con un 34.4%, España es el cuarto país europeo con mayor brecha salarial entre hombres y mujeres," 1 January 2010. Accessed 13 March 2015. http://www.adecco .es/_data/NotasPrensa/pdf/197.pdf.

AFL-CIO. *Death on the Job: The Toll of Neglect – 20th edition*. Washington, DC: American Federation of Labor and Congress of Industrial Organizations, 2011.

Aglietta, Michel. *Regulación y crisis del capitalismo*. Madrid: Siglo XXI Editores, 1979.

Aguilar, Alonso. "En torno a la crisis actual." In *La crisis actual del capitalismo*, 13–40. Mexico: Comité Coordinador del Centro Mexicano de Estudios Sociales, Siglo XXI Editores, 2011.

Alianza Global Jus Semper. "Gráficas de Brecha Salarial Manufacturera para Brasil frente a economías desarrolladas y 'emergentes' seleccionadas, con datos salariales y PPC disponibles (1996–2009)." Accessed 2 February 2015. http://www.jussemper.org/ Inicio/Recursos/Recursos%20Laborales/GBS/Resources/GrafsbrechasBras2006.pdf.

Alves, Giovanni. "Crise estrutural do capital: trabalho imaterial e modelo de competência, notas dialéticas." In *Trabalho e educação. Contradições do capitalismo global*, edited by Francisco Luiz Corsi *et al.*, 47–81. São Paulo: Editora Praxis, 2006.

———. *Dimensões da reestruturação produtiva.Ensaios de sociologia do trabalho*. São Paulo: Editora Praxis, 2007.

———. *A condição da proletariedade*. Londrina, São Paulo: Editora Praxis, 2009.

———. "Crise de valorização e desmedida do capital. Breve ensaio sobre a natureza da crise estrutural do capital." In *Capital trabajo y nueva organización obrera*, edited by Esthela Gutiérrez, Dídimo Castillo and Adrián Sotelo, 15–39. Mexico: Siglo XXI Editores, 2011.

Amorim, Henrique. *Trabalho imaterial: Marx e o debate contemporánio*. São Paulo: FAPESP, Annablume Editora, 2009.

Anderson, Perry. "Balance del neoliberalismo." In *Pos-neoliberalismo. As políticas sociais e o estado democrático*, edited by Emir Sader and Pablo Gentili, 9–23. São Paulo: Paz e Terra, 1995.

Antunes, Ricardo. *Los sentidos del trabajo*. Buenos Aires: Ediciones Herramienta, 2005.

———. "La dialéctica entre el trabajo concreto y el trabajo abstracto." *Revista Herramienta* (Buenos Aires) 44 (2010). Accessed 9 June 2014. http://www.herramienta .com.ar/revista-herramienta-n-44/la-dialectica-entre-el-trabajo-concreto-y-el-trabajo-abstracto.

———. *O continente do labor*. São Paulo: Boitempo Editorial, 2011.

———. *The Meanings of Work: Essay on the Affirmation and Negation of Work*, translated by Elizabeth Molinari. Leiden: Brill, 2013.

Arriola, Joaquín and Luciano Vasapollo. *Flexibles y precarios. La opresión del trabajo en el nuevo capitalismo europeo*. Madrid: El Viejo Topo, 2003.

Arze Vargas, Carlos. "Aumento salarial: ¿garantizar la reproducción de la fuerza de trabajo o el aumento de la explotación?" *Rebelión*, 22 April 2011. Accessed 8 March 2015, http://www.rebelion.org/docs/126780.pdf. [Originally published in La Paz: Centro de Estudios para el Desarrollo Laboral y Agrario, 2010].

Askenazy, Philippe, Thomas Coutrot, Henri Sterdyniak and André Orléan. *Manifeste d'économistes atterrés. Crise et dettes en Europe. Dix fausses évidences, 22 mesures en débat pour sortir de l'impasse*. Paris: Les Liens qui Libèrent, 2010.

Bagú, Sergio. *Economía de la sociedad colonial. Ensayo de historia comparada de América Latina*. Mexico: Editorial Grijalbo, Consejo Nacional para la Cultura y las Artes, 1992.

Bambirra, Vania. *Teoría de la dependencia: una anticrítica*. Mexico: Era, 1978.

Bell, Daniel. *The Coming of Post-industrial Society: A Venture in Social Forecasting*. New York: Basic Books, 1973.

Bihr, Alain. "Las formas concretas del trabajo abstracto." *Revista Herramiento* (Buenos Aires) 44 (2010): 29–37.

Blomström, Magnus and Björn Hettne. *La teoría del desarrollo en transición*. Mexico: Fondo de Cultura Económia, 1990.

Braverman, Harry. *Labor and Monopoly Capitalism*. New York: Monthly Review, 1974.

Callinicos, Alex. *Imperialism and Global Political Economy*. Cambridge: Polity Press, 2009.

Castells, Manuel. *The Information Age: Economy, Society and Culture. Volume I: The Rise of the Network Society – 2nd edition*. Oxford: Blackwell, 2002.

Castillo Fernández, Dídimo. *Los nuevos trabajadores precarios*. Mexico: Miguel Ángel Porrúa, Universidad Autónoma del Estado de México, 2009.

Chossudovsky, Michel. *The Globalisation of Poverty: Impacts of IMF and World Bank Reforms*. London: Zed Books, 1999.

Coriat, Benjamín. *Pensar al revés. Trabajo y organización de la empresa japonesa*. Mexico: Siglo XXI Editores, 1992.

Dal Rosso, Sadi. *Mais Trabalho! A intensificação do labor na sociedade contemporânea*. São Paulo: Boitempo, 2008.

Drucker, Peter. *The Age of Discontinuity*. New York: Harper & Row, 1969.

Echeverría, Bolívar. *Valor de uso y utopía – 2nd edition*. Mexico: Siglo XXI Editores, 2010.

ECLAC. "Commodity Price Rises and Volatility Pose a Challenge to Latin American Economies" (press release), 21 May 2011, accessed 20 October 2014, http://www.cepal.org/cgi-bin/getProd.asp?xml=/prensa/noticias/comunicados/7/43527/P43527.xml&xsl=/prensa/tpl-i/p6f.xsl&base=/prensa/tpl/top-bottom.xslt.

ECLAC. *Economic Survey of Latin America and the Caribbean 2010–2011: International Integration and Macroeconomic Policy Challenges Amid Global Turmoil*. Santiago de

Chile, United Nations, November 2011. Accessed 25 January 2015. http://repositorio
.cepal.org/bitstream/11362/1075/86/2010-2011_en.pdf.

ECLAC. *Latin America and the Caribbean in the World Economy 2010–2011: The Region in
the Decade of the Emerging Economies*, Santiago de Chile, United Nations, 2011.

Economist Intelligence Unit. "Estados Unidos: ¿fin de la crisis?" *La Jornada*, 9 August
2011. Accessed 24 March 2015. http://www.jornada.unam.mx/2011/08/09/economia/
030n1eco.

Emmanuel, Arghiri. *Unequal Exchange: A Study of the Imperialism of Trade*, translated
by Brian Pearce. London: Monthly Review, 1972.

Emmanuel, Arghiri, Charles Bettelheim, Samir Amin and Christian Palloix.
"Imperialismo y comercio desigual" (special issue). *Cuadernos de Pasado y Presente
24* (Córdoba), 1971.

Fajnzylber, Fernando. *La industrialización trunca en América Latina – 4th edition*.
Mexico: Nueva Imagen, 1988.

———. "Industrialización en América Latina. De la 'caja negra' al 'casillero vacío'."
Cuadernos de la CEPAL 60 (Santiago de Chile: Naciones Unidas), 1990.

Fernández Durán, Ramón. "Profundización de la Europa del capital." *Rebelión*, 22 July
2011. Accessed 19 December 2014. http://www.rebelion.org/noticia.php?id=110089
[Originally published in *Revista Pueblos 42* (June 2010)].

Fernández Steinko, Armando. *Clase, trabajo y ciudadanía. Introducción a la existencia
social*. Madrid: Biblioteca Nueva, 2004.

Fontes, Virgínia. *O capital-imperialismo.Teoria e história*. Rio de Janeiro: Editora UFRJ,
2010.

Forneo, José Luis. "Un 35% de los asalariados rumanos ganan menos de 170 euros netos
al mes." *Rebelión*, 26 March 2011. Accessed 8 March 2015. http://www.rebelion.org/
noticia.php?id=125139.

Frangakis, Marcia. "How the EU Made the Greek Crisis Worse," *Counterpunch*, 15–17
July 2011. Accessed 23 March 2015. http://www.counterpunch.org/2011/07/15/
how-the-eu-made-the-greek-crisis-worse/.

Gambina, Julio C. "Economía a fines del 2011." *Rebelión*, 20 December 2011. Accessed
21 January 2015, http://www.rebelion.org/noticia.php?id=141613.

Goldstein, Fred. *"Capitalism at a Dead-End: Job Destruction, Overproduction and Crisis
in the High Tech Era: A Marxist View."* Workers World, 11 June, 2011. Accessed 21 July
2014. http://www.workers.org/ebooks/CapitalismDeadEnd.pdf.

Gorz, André. *Miseria del presente, riqueza de lo posible*. Buenos Aires: Paidós, 1998.

———. *O Imaterial: conhecimento, valor e capital*. São Paulo: Annablume Editora,
2005.

Gutiérrez Garza, Esthela and Edgar González Gaudiano. *De las teorías del desarrollo al
desarrollo sustentable*. México: Universidad Autónoma de Nuevo León, Siglo XXI
Editores, 2010.

Habermas, Jürgen. *The Theory of Communicative Action. Volume 2: Lifeworld and System: A Critique of Functionalist Reason.* Boston: Beacon Press, 1989.

Hardt, Michael and Antonio Negri. *Empire.* London: Harvard University Press, 2002.

Harman, Chris. "Economic Crisis: Capitalism Exposed," *Socialist Review*, February 2008, accessed 20 October 2014, https://www.marxists.org/archive/harman/2008/02/crisis2.htm.

Harvey, David. *El nuevo imperialismo.* Madrid: Akal, 2003.

Hirata, Helena. "¿Sociedad del ocio? El trabajo se intensificó." *Página 12* (Buenos Aires), 2 January 2001. Accessed 23 November 2014. http://www.pagina12.com.ar/2001/01-02/01-02-12/pag11.htm.

Husson, Michel. "Breakup of the Eurozone?" *Counterpunch*, 27–29 May 2011. Accessed 23 March 2015. http://www.counterpunch.org/2011/05/27/breakup-of-the-eurozone/.

———. "A Crisis without End." *International Viewpoint*, 8 August 2011. Accessed 6 April 2015. http://www.internationalviewpoint.org/spip.php?article2236.

Ibarra, David. *Ensayos sobre economía mexicana.* Mexico: Fondo de Cultural Económica, 2005.

ILO. *Global Wage Report 2010/11: Wage Policies in Times of Crisis.* Geneva: International Labour Office, 2010. Accessed 8 March 2015. http://www.ilo.org/wcmsp5/groups/public/---dgreports/---dcomm/---publ/documents/publication/wcms_145265.pdf.

Jalife-Rahme, Alfredo. *El fin de una era. Turbulencias de la globalización.* Mexico: Orfila, 2007.

———. *El híbrido mundo multipolar. Un enfoque multidimensional.* Mexico: Orfila, 2010.

Katz, Claudio. "Discusiones sobre el declive de Estados Unidos." *Rebelión*, 30 July 2011. Accessed 14 March 2015. http://www.rebelion.org/noticia.php?id=133194.

———. "Los cambios en la rivalidad interimperial." *Rebelión*, 24 July 2011. Accessed 19 December 2014. http://www.rebelion.org/noticia.php?id=132805.

Kurz, Robert, Norbert Trenkle and Ernst Lohoff. "Manifesto against Labour." *Krisis: Kritik der Warengesellschaft*, 31 December 1999. Accessed 28 September 2014. http://www.krisis.org/1999/manifesto-against-labour.

Lazzarato, Maurizio and Antonio Negri. *Trabajo inmaterial. Formas de vida y producción de subjetividad. Rebelión*, 2 December 2002. Accessed 11 October 2014. http://www.rebelion.org/noticia.php?id=121986. [Originally published in Rio de Janeiro: DP&A Editora, 2001].

———. "Immaterial Labour." *The Generation-Online Blog*, translated by Paul Colilli and Ed Emery. Accessed 15 May 2014. http://www.generation-online.org/c/fcimmateriallabour3.htm.

Lessa, Sergio. *Trabalho e proletariado no capitalismcontemporâneo.* São Paulo: Cortez Editora, 2007.

Llopis, Enric. "La economía sumergida se dispara con la crisis." *Rebelión*, 12 August 2011. Accessed 13 March 2015. http://www.rebelion.org/noticia.php?id=133888.

Lozano, Luis *et al. De llantas y atropellos. Trabajo, salario, productividad y derechos laborales en la industria llantera mexicana*. Mexico: Centro de Análisis Multidisciplinario – Universidad Nacional Autónoma de México (CAM-UNAM), Sindicato Nacional de Trabajadores de General Tire de México, 2009.

Luce, Mathias. "La expansión del subimperialismo brasileño." *Rebelión*, 12 April 2008. Accessed 23 November 2014. http://www.rebelion.org/noticia.php?id=76977.

Lukács, György. *Ontology of the Social Being. Volume 3: Labour*. London: Merlin Press, 1980.

Marini, Ruy Mauro. *Dialéctica de la dependencia*. Ciudad de México: Era, 1973.

———. *Subdesarrollo y revolución – 5ᵃ edición*. Ciudad de México: Siglo XXI Editores, 1974.

———. "La acumulación capitalista mundial y el subimperialismo." *Cuadernos Políticos* (Ciudad de México) *12* (April–June 1977): 21–39.

———. "Estado y crisis en Brasil." *Cuadernos Políticos* (Ciudad de México) *13* (July–September 1977): 76–84.

———. "Las razones del neodesarrollismo (respuesta a Fernando Enrique Cardoso y José Serra)." *Revista Mexicana de Sociología* (Ciudad de México) XL (1978): 57–106.

———. "El ciclo del capital en la economía dependiente." In *Mercado y dependencia*, edited by Úrsula Oswald, 37–55. Mexico: Nueva Imagen, 1979.

———. "Plusvalía extraordinaria y acumulación de capital." *Cuadernos Políticos* (Ciudad de México) 20 (April–June 1979): 18–39.

———. "Preface." In *México, dependencia y modernización*, written by Adrián Sotelo Valencia, 9–12. Ciudad de México: El Caballito, 1990.

———. "El concepto de trabajo productivo, nota metodológica." *Archivo de Ruy Mauro Marini*, 1993. Accessed 16 April 2015. http://www.marini-escritos.unam.mx/078_trabajo_productivo.html.

———. "Introducción: la década de 1970 revisitada." In *La teoría social latinoamericana. Volume III, La centralidad del marxismo*, edited by Ruy Mauro Marini and Márgara Millán. Ciudad de México: El Caballito, 1995.

———. "Proceso y tendencias de la globalización capitalista." In *La teoría social latinoamericana. Volume IV, Cuestiones contemporáneas*, edited by Ruy Mauro Marini and Márgara Millán, 49–68. Ciudad de México: El Caballito, 1996.

Martins, Carlos Eduardo. *Globalização, dependência e neoliberalismo na América Latina*. Rio de Janeiro: Boitempo Editorial, 2011.

Marx, Karl. *Capital – Volume I*. New York: International Publishers, 1974.

———. "Economic and Philosophical Manuscripts (1844)." In *Marx Early Writings*, translated by Rodney Livingstone and Gregor Benton, 279–400. London: Penguin, 1975.

———. *The Poverty of Philosophy*. Moscow: Progress Publishers, 1975.

———. *Capital – Volume III*. New York: International Publishers, 1977.

————. *Capital – Volume II*. New York: International Publishers, 1984.

————. "Results of the Immediate Process of Production." In *Capital – Volume I*, 948–1084. London: Penguin, 1990.

————. *Grundrisse: Foundations of the Critique of Political Economy (Rough Draft)*. London: Penguin Books, 1993.

————. *El capital, Libro III*. Mexico: Fondo de Cultural Económica, 2000.

Méda, Dominique. *El trabajo. Un valor en extinción*. Barcelona: Gedisa, 1998.

Mészáros, István. *Beyond Capital: Towards a Theory of Transition*. New York: Monthly Review, 1995.

————. *Socialism or Barbarism: From the "American Century" to the Crossroads*. New York: Monthly Review, 2001.

————. *Más allá del capital. Hacia una teoría de la transición*. Caracas: Vadell Hermanos Editores, 2001.

Moreira, Jorge. "La batalla contra el gobierno antidemocrático del estado de Wisconsin." *Rebelión*, 28 February 2011. Accessed 28 September 2014. http://www.rebelion.org/noticia.php?id=123317.

Munevar, Daniel. "Alzas en los precios de alimentos. Una mirada desde América Latina. Documento de Discusión 1." *Rebelion*, June 2011. Comité pour l'Annulation de la Dette du Tiers Monde. Accessed 20 October 2014. http://www.rebelion.org/docs/131093.pdf.

Osorio, Jaime. *Explotación redoblada y actualidad de la revolución. Refundación societal, rearticulación popular y nuevo autoritarismo*. Mexico: Editorial Itaca, Unidad Xochimilco – Universidad Autónoma Metropolitana, 2009.

Pérez, Andrés. "La crisis de suicidios en France Telecom se reabre trágicamente." *Rebelión*, 28 April 2011. Accessed 1 December 2014. http://www.rebelion.org/noticia.php?id=127314.

Piqueras, Andrés. "Cuando la 'guerra de clase' se hace guerra en los campos de batalla.' *Rebelión*, 12 May 2011. Accessed 24 March 2015. http://www.rebelion.org/noticia.php?id=128167.

Rifkin, Jeremy. "Tiempo libre para disfrutarlo o hacer filas de desempleados," edited by Luis Álvarez, *Un mundo sin trabajo*, 15–49. Mexico: Dríada, 2003.

Roelandts, Marcel. *Capitalism & Economic Crises*. Last accessed 22 June 2015. http://www.capitalism-and-crisis.info/en.

Roitman Rosenmann, Marcos. "¡Por favour, salven a la Unión Europea y el euro!" *La Jornada*, 23 July 2011, accessed 22 July 2015, http://www.jornada.unam.mx/2011/07/23/index.php?section=opinion&article=018a2pol.

Rosdolsky, Roman. *Génesis y estructura de* El capital *de Marx. Estudios sobre los Grundrisse*. Ciudad de México: Siglo XXI Editores, 1978.

Salles, Severo. *Carlos Marx y Rosa Luxemburgo. La acumulación de capital en debate*. Buenos Aires: Peña Lillo, Ediciones Continente, 2009.

Samath, Feizal. "Industria de la vestimenta corteja a mujeres." *Rebelión*, 13 February 2011. Accessed 8 March 2015. http://www.rebelion.org/noticia.php?id=122341.

Santos, Boaventura de Sousa. *Refundación del Estado en América Latina. Perspectivas desde una epistemología del sur.* Ciudad de México: Universidad de los Andes, Siglo del Hombre Editores, Siglo XXI Editores, 2010.

———. "Public Sphere and Epistemologies of the South." *Africa Development* 37(1) (2012): 43–67.

Seda-Irizarry, Ian J. "Estados Unidos y la crisis capitalista" (entrevista a Richard Wolff). *Rebelión*, 2 August 2010. Accessed 7 March 2015. http://www.rebelion.org/noticia .php?id=110683.

Sennett, Richard. *The Corrosion of Character: The Personal Consequences of Work in the New Capitalism.* London: W.W. Norton & Co., 1998.

Shaikh, Anwar. "The First Great Depression of the 21st Century." *Socialist Register* 47 (2011): 44–63.

Sotelo Valencia, Adrián. *La reestruturación del mundo del trabajo, superexplotación y nuevos paradigmas de la organización del trabajo.* Mexico: Universidad Obrera de México, Editorial Ithaca, Escuela Nacional para Trabajadores (ENAT, Plantel Morelia), 2003.

———. *Desindustrialización y crisis del neoliberalismo. Maquiladoras y telecomunicaciones.* México: Plaza y Valdés, 2004.

———. *El mundo del trabajo en tensión. Flexibilidad laboral y fractura social en la década de 2000.* Mexico: Plaza y Valdés Editores, Facultad de Ciencias Políticas y Sociales – Universidad Nacional Autónoma de México, 2007.

———. *A reestruturação do mundo do trabalho. Superexploração e novos paradigmas de organização do trabalho.* Minas Gerais: Editora da Universidade Federal de Uberlândia, 2009.

———. *Crisis capitalista y desmedida del valor: un enfoque desde los Grundrisse.* Mexico: Editorial Ítaca, Facultad de Ciencias Políticas y Sociales – Universidad Nacional Autónoma de México, 2010.

———. "Grecia: preludio de la crisis global del capital." *Rebelión*, 16 May 2011. Accessed 24 March 2015. http://www.rebelion.org/noticia.php?id=105954.

Stehr, Nico. *Knowledge Societies.* Thousand Oaks, California: Sage Publications, 1994.

Valenzuela Feijóo, José Carlos. *Sociología de la corrupción. Alianzas, corrupción y conciencia de clase* [mimeo].

Vence, Xavier. "Da burbulla financiero-alimentaria ás novas burbullas especulativas da enerxía e dos alimentos." In *Cadernos de formación* (June). Galicia: CIG, Fesga, 2008.

Weller, Jürgen, ed. *El nuevo scenario laboral latinoamericano. Regulación, protección y políticas activas en los mercados de trabajo.* Buenos Aires: CEPAL, Siglo XXI Editores, 2009.

Online Articles

"Alemania sufre un parón en el segunda trimestre de 2011." *El País*, 16 August 2011. Accessed 30 March 2015. http://economia.elpais.com/economia/2011/08/16/actualidad/1313479975_850215.html.

"El Parlamento griego apoya las nuevas medidas de austeridad." *La Jornada*, 22 June 2011. Accessed 24 March 2015. http://www.jornada.unam.mx/2011/06/22/economia/034n2eco.

"En peligro, la economía mundial: Zoellick." *La Jornada*, 14 August 2011. Accessed 24 March 2015. http://www.jornada.unam.mx:8810/2011/08/14/economia/027n1eco.

"El Senado de Estados Unidos aprueba la subida del techo de deuda para evitar la quiebra." *El País*, 2 August 2011. Accessed 24 March 2015. http://internacional.elpais.com/internacional/2011/08/02/actualidad/1312236006_850215.html.

"Global Wealth 2011: Shaping a New Tomorrow." *The Boston Consulting Group*, 31 May 2011. Accessed 29 August 2015. https://www.bcgperspectives.com/content/articles/financial_institutions_pricing_global_wealth_2011_shaping_new_tomorrow/?chapter=2#chapter2_section3.

"Grecia aprueba los recortes y libera el camino para recibir la ayuda de la UE y el FMI." *El País*, 29 June 2011. Accessed 24 March 2015. http://economia.elpais.com/economia/2011/06/29/actualidad/1309332773_850215.html.

"Italia golpea a los más débiles para reducir su déficit en 79.000 millones." *El País*, 15 July 2011. Accessed 24 March 2015. http://elpais.com/diario/2011/07/15/economia/1310680806_850215.html.

"La débil actividad económica interna propició menor inflación." *La Jornada*, 10 June 2011. Accessed 20 October 2014. http://www.jornada.unam.mx/2011/06/10/economia/029n1eco.

"Obama promulga ley para evitar suspensión de pagos." *El Universal*, 2 August 2011. Accessed 24 March 2015. http://www.eluniversal.com.mx/notas/783126.html.

"Secuelas de la crisis golpean hoy a Europe." *El Universal*, 11 July 2011. Accessed 23 March 2015. http://www.eluniversal.com.mx/notas/780376.html.

"Standard & Poor's priva a EE UU de la triple A por su "improvisada política fiscal." *El País*, 6 August 2011. Accessed 21 July 2014. http://economia.elpais.com/economia/2011/08/06/actualidad/1312615974_850215.html.

Index

abstract labour   4–5, 7, 16–18, 34–36, 41,
    46–47
    crisis of   33, 41–42
accidents, work-related   80
accumulation   22, 28, 51, 53, 62, 73, 77,
    83, 89–90, 94–95, 97, 107, 115, 131,
    141–142
    buttress capital   62
advanced capitalist countries   4, 6, 73, 77,
    81, 84, 105, 108, 110, 115, 121–125, 132,
    134–35
AFL-CIO   80, 137
Africa   2, 13, 85, 124–125, 132, 143
age   2, 12, 36, 77, 138
Aglietta   26, 34, 37, 47, 137
agriculture   90, 92, 101, 116, 138
Alianza Global Jus Semper   99, 115, 137
Alves, Giovanni   13–14, 36, 39, 41–42, 46,
    78–79, 83, 137
Anderson, Perry   90–91
antipodes   5, 9, 11, 13, 15, 17, 19–20, 56
    labour-capital   12
Antunes, Ricardo   13–17, 39, 60, 100, 137
appropriation   39, 115–116, 133
Argentina   50, 68, 93, 101, 119
Arrighi, Giovanni   69, 137, 139
Asia   2, 85, 118, 124–125
austerity   120, 127, 129, 131–132
Austria   85, 117, 119, 121, 127
average labour productivity   109
average rate of exploitation   39
average rate of profit   36, 40, 42, 62
average wages   116–117, 119, 120

Vânia Bambirra   73–74, 95, 138
banks   53, 57, 106, 135
Bell, Daniel   12
Bolivia   115, 116
book   22, 42, 90–91, 96, 122, 131, 134
boom   111–112
branches   28, 34, 35, 37, 48, 62
Brazil   67–70, 74–75, 77, 89, 93, 99, 100–101,
    114, 115, 116, 125, 141
Buenos Aires   14, 17, 22, 27, 43, 75, 137, 139,
    140, 142–143

Capital   40, 54, 142
capital   3–6, 18–44, 48–49, 51–54, 56–57, 60,
    70–72, 83, 94, 108, 135, 141–43
    accumulation of   5, 10, 12, 22, 27, 32–33,
        67, 70–74, 80, 83
    centralisation of   48, 53, 107
    circulation of   24, 32, 58
    concentration of   91, 95
    constant and variable   5, 21, 24–27, 32, 43
    cycle of capital   53, 74, 91, 99
    elements of   60, 92
    destructiveness of   14, 16
    developed   48
    fictitious capital   4, 5, 17, 40, 48, 52,
        55–56, 59, 60, 106
    financial   32, 41, 78
    foreign   74, 90–91, 101
    global   40, 78–79, 84, 87, 129, 131
    globalised   4, 66, 82, 87, 105–106
    imperialist   88
    invested   43, 55
    merchant   40, 73
    money   40, 59, 73
    neoliberal   131
    organic composition of   32, 41, 77, 108,
        110–112, 114–115
    parasitic   131
    productive   40, 59, 131
    self-expansion of   29, 30
    self-valorisation of   4, 17–18, 20–24, 28, 31,
        38, 48, 83–84, 107
    social   17–18
    social metabolism of   20, 44, 52, 60
    speculative finance   60
    technical composition of   48, 114
    technological   78
    turnover of   24
    value composition of   71, 93
capitalism   1–2, 10–11, 34, 41, 47, 59, 61, 67, 77,
    82–83, 93, 95–99, 100, 108, 123, 131, 133,
    135, 138
    advanced   5–6, 86, 88, 94, 96–98, 102–103,
        106, 109, 118, 120, 126
    dependent   5–6, 37, 51, 68, 90, 93, 97–98,
        105–106, 110